Also by Loren Mayshark

Death: An Exploration

Academic Betrayal: The Bullying of a Graduate Student

Inside the Chinese Wine Industry

The Past, Present, and Future of Wine in China

Loren Mayshark

All Rights Reserved

Published by Red Scorpion Press

www.redscropionpress.com

PO Box 289

Bemus Point, New York 14712

Copyright © 2018 Loren Mayshark

This book is protected under the copyright laws of the United States of America. Any reproduction or unauthorized use of the material or artwork herein is prohibited without the express written consent of the author.

To my girls: Cornelia and Maya. Without your love and support I would not have completed this book. You make my life richer.

"Wine brings to light the hidden secrets of the soul, gives being to our hopes, bids the coward flight, drives dull care away, and teaches new means for the accomplishment of our wishes."

-Horace

Table of Contents

Timeline of Chinese Eras xi

Timeline of History of Wine in China xii

PREFACE xiii

CHAPTER I: Introduction 1

CHAPTER II: A Brief History of China While Tracing the Origins
of Wine Consumption 5

    Wine in China BCE 6

    The Significance of the Han Dynasty 8

    The Rise of Grape Wine During the T'ang Dynasty 12

    China in the 1800s 16

    China in the 1900s 17

CHAPTER III: The Turn to Spirits and Other Types of Alcohol
in China 18

    Other Types of "Wine" Consumed in China 20

    Vitis Vinifera in China 21

CHAPTER IV: Factors That Affected the Rise in Consumption and Production of Grape Wine in China 25

    Emperor Kangxi Sets a Precedent for Wine in Modern China 25

    Wine in Communist China 28

    Li Peng's Proclamation is the Spark that Ignites the Wine Industry.......... 30

    The 1855 Classification in Bordeaux 33

    How 1855 Distinguished Bordeaux 35

    Status and "Face" in Chinese Culture.. 37

    How the 1855 Classification Relates to the Wine Industry in China......... 38

CHAPTER V: China's Forays into the International Wine Scene............. 41

    Why has the Chinese Wine Industry Grown so Significantly in the Last Twenty Years? 45

    Learning from the Wine Venture of a Foreign Businessman in China....... 48

CHAPTER VI: Counterfeit Wines and Appellation..................................... 52

    Koch Experiences Counterfeiting Up Close and Personal 52

    In China, Fake Wine Has Become a Thriving Industry............................. 56

    Nick Bartman's Big Find.. 59

    The Fake Wine Continues to Flow 63

    Appellation in China 63

CHAPTER VII: Global Considerations Regarding Chinese Wines........... 67

    Importing... 67

    Exporting... 70

    Shipping Wine to and From China 71

Foreign Businessmen in China 72

Why Does China Export so Little Wine? 76

Why Is There Not a Lot of Wine Exported to the
United States and Europe? 78

CHAPTER VIII: Wine Tourism in China 81

Wine Bars 81

Wine Bars in Hong Kong 82

Wine Bars on the Mainland 83

A Final Word on Wine Bars 84

The Wine Regions of China 84

CHAPTER IX: The Future of the Chinese Wine Industry 98

How the 2012 Crackdown has Changed the Chinese Wine Market 98

Electronic and Mobile Commerce May Define the Future of
Chinese Wine Consumption 101

How Good are Chinese Wines? 105

Titans in the Wine Industry Turn their Attention to China 108

The Future and Hong Kong 115

The Next Half Century of Chinese Wine 122

The Ascent of Sparkling and White Wine 125

China's Infatuation with Icewine 129

Other Factors Affecting the Future of Chinese Wine Production 131

The Future of the United States and Chinese Wines 133

CHAPTER X: Conclusion 135

APPENDIX 138

BIBLIOGRAPHY 140

ACKNOWLEDGEMENTS 152

ABOUT THE AUTHOR 154

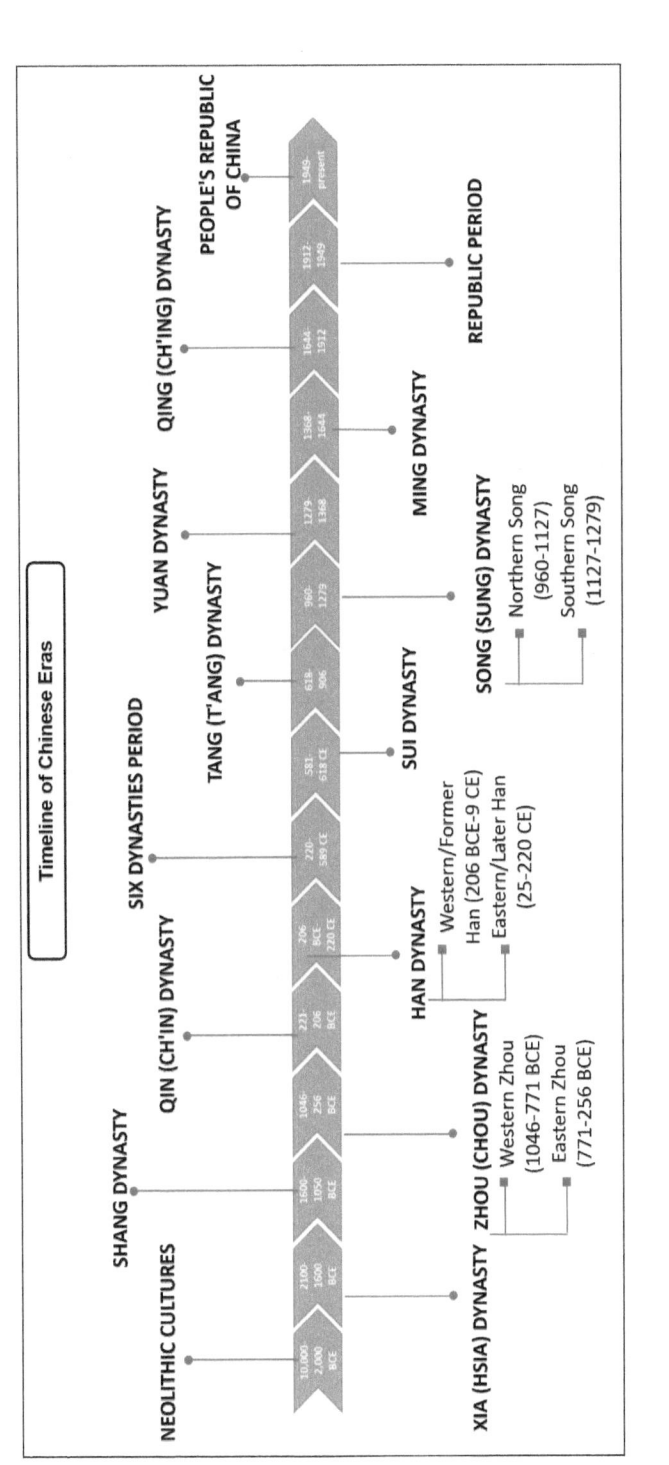

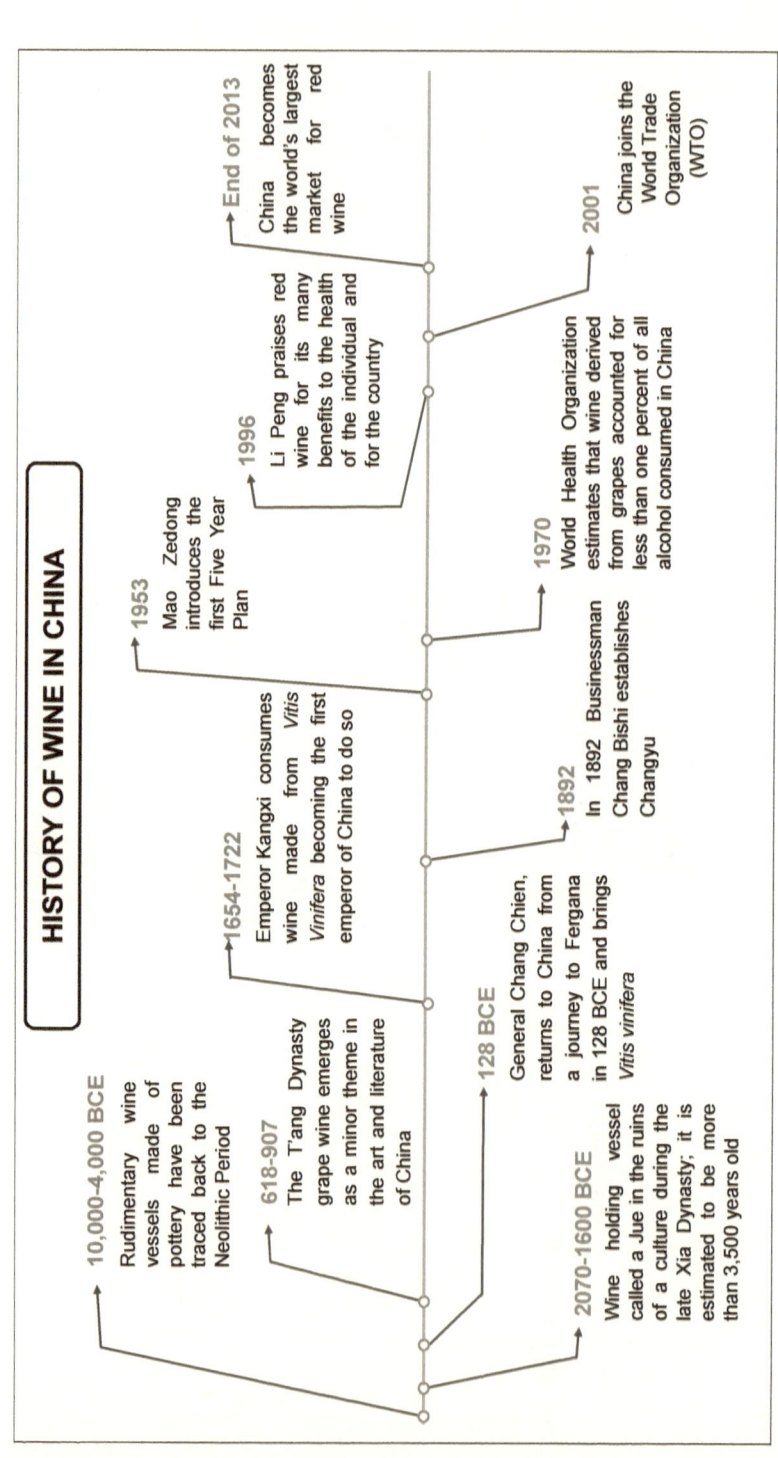

Preface

My parents, when I was no older than six, started taking me to New York City, usually to visit my father's friend who lived in a variety of places over the years in Manhattan. His residences went from downtown to eventually Lincoln Towers. On one of these visits, I went to Chinatown: I was hooked. Whenever we visited the Big Apple and I was asked where I wanted to go, I would say Chinatown. A lifelong fascination with China emerged.

In 2005, as a twenty-something while employed at Fisherman's Grotto in San Francisco, I worked with many Chinese women and men learning more about the language and culture. I also made several trips up to Napa and Sonoma valleys to taste wines and visit vineyards to learn about wine and the process of making an enjoyable drink and savor the experience. This had a profound impact on my life. I not only became more familiar with Chinese culture, but I developed a familiarity with wine production.

In 2007, I moved to Long Island and worked a season as a field worker at Paumanok Vineyards on the North Fork. I learned about shoot positioning suckering, and later I would trim leaves and even remove bunches of grapes. I worked with an almost entirely

Guatemalan staff while I was there which also proved to be a transformative experience, because I saw the agricultural side of winemaking first-hand and had the unique opportunity to observe all facets of wine production. This opportunity gave me a newfound reverence for what it takes to make a bottle of wine.

At the same time, I was bartending at the Jedediah Hawkins House in Jamesport, New York. This was an old Captain's Manor that had been restored into a bed-and-breakfast. In the restaurant portion, celebrity chefs Tom Schaudel and Mike Ross helped to shape the cuisine around local sustainable foods with a wine list of more than one hundred wines. At least 60% of the bottles were Long Island wines. Working with these brilliant chefs and learning about the wine industry on Long Island gave me a deeper appreciation for wine/food pairings and local sustainable agriculture. These experiences continued to shape my life. I attended an MA History program in New York City after that and few years thereafter, I went back home and worked for a home produce delivery, which was essentially a type of CSA (Community Supported Agriculture) in Chautauqua County. Around this time is when I began working as a freelance writer.

As a freelance writer, I wrote dozens of articles about food and drink. After starting a career as a bartender in San Francisco and working in mostly high-end restaurants from coast to coast for a decade, I have continued to enjoy wine and increase my knowledge of wine and the wine industry. This is something that I still enjoy as I develop my palate and passion. Freelance writing offered a new way for me to enjoy and explore wine.

While working as a freelance writer, I started writing for an online Chinese travel blog and learning about the Chinese wine industry. I became completely fascinated with the subject. It was amazing to see Chinese history and culture through the prism of wine, and from that viewpoint something emerged that became a life-changing obsession. I read everything possible about Chinese wine and wrote about it for a couple different outlets. This was the seed of the book that you're about to read. I was motivated because I noticed that although there are some great books about certain aspects of the industry, there is no full comprehensive overview, in the English language, of the Chinese wine industry that not only takes into account its unique history, but also looks at where it is today, and how it's changing so dynamically. It was something that started to get me thinking about the future of Chinese wine and the ramifications of its growth because China is a sleeping dragon that has awoken to shake the wine-drinking world.

CHAPTER I

Introduction

Few things signal civilization and sophistication more than enjoying a fine wine with an excellent meal. It may be asserted that China is the world's oldest continuous civilization. One of the features of its culture is that Chinese cuisine serves up superb meals. Until recently, however, fine wines have been absent there, at least wine made from the noble grape.

In many ways, we live in a golden age for wine. The wine world has many exciting new wrinkles from fancy new mobile applications to devices that allow us to extract a glass of wine from a bottle and then return it to the cellar to rest for a couple of years without changing the character of the wine. With all the current trends and innovations, it is the best time to enjoy wine. This is certainly a special age, in the words of renowned wine critic Jancis Robinson: "The irony is that just as the difference in price between the best and worst wines is greater than it has ever been, the difference in quality is narrower than ever before."[1]

---

[1] Quoted in George M. Taber, *A Toast to Bargain Wines: How Innovators, Iconoclasts, and Winemaking Revolutionaries Are Changing the Way the World Drinks*, 1st Scribner ed (New York: Scribner, 2011), 1.

Perhaps one of the most pervasive reasons for this truism, which Robinson so eloquently captured, is the globalization of the wine industry. One cannot fully understand the global wine industry of today without developing a deeper understanding of its largest and fastest growing player: China.

Though starting relatively late historically with grape wine production and consumption, China has been catching up quickly. China's role in the global wine industry continues to grow at an astonishing pace. Wine consumption in China doubled between 2008 and 2013 when China became the fifth largest consumer of wine in the world. At the end of 2013, China became the world's largest market for red wine, and China is projected to become the second most valuable market for wine in the world by 2020 (behind the U.S.), which will have a profound impact on various aspects of the global wine industry.[2] These are significant statistics for anyone who has a serious interest in the global wine industry.

To feed the rapidly rising consumption, the domestic production in China has also increased at an amazing rate. China now has more than seven hundred vineyards, compared to 240 in 1995.[3] As of 2018, China is projected to have the second largest area of wine grapes planted in the world and to be the seventh largest producer of wine.[4]

---

[2] Vinexpo Newsroom, "China Is a Leading Wine Market of the Future," *Vinexpo Newsroom - Wine & Spirits News by Vinexpo* (blog), April 4, 2017, https://www.vinexpo-newsroom.com/china-is-a-leading-wine-market-of-the-future/.

[3] Suzanne Mustacich, *Thirsty Dragon: China's Lust for Bordeaux and the Threat to the World's Best Wines*, First edition (New York: Henry Holt and Company, 2015), 56.

[4] "State of the Vitiviniculture World Market" (International Organisation of Wine and Vine (OIV), April 2018), http://www.oiv.int/public/medias/5958/oiv-state-of-the-vitiviniculture-world-market-april-2018.pdf.

While wine has deep roots in Western culture, China has a rich history of wine production which dates back to millennia before Christ. However, it must be stressed that this tradition is almost exclusively rice wine. The production and mass consumption of grape wine is a recent phenomenon in China. A 2015 poll found that 96 percent of young adults in China select wine as their favored alcoholic beverage.[5] This book examines the development of the Chinese wine industry in a historical context and explains how the Chinese grape wine industry has exploded in the last two decades. We will explore the fascination with European Grapes in China and the explosion of the import and consumption of *Vitis vinifera* (the most important wine-grape species in the world) in China and the historical precedent for that. We will attempt to answer burning questions such as: What changed to make China wine-crazy? How can a tourist enjoy unique wine experiences in China? Why is mass wine production and consumption a modern phenomenon? Why are there not a lot of Chinese wines exported to the United States and Europe?

In 1919, wine expert André Simon stated, "In the old world, winemaking is an art; in the new world, it is an industry."[6] Today, many have tried to meld the two with some intriguing results. This brings us to some other interesting questions: What are the economic dimensions of the wine industry in China? What does the future hold

---

[5] Can Akalin and Lawrence Lazar, *Wine in China: Insights on a Burgeoning Industry in an e/m Commerce Context*, 2nd edition, Kindle Edition, (CreateSpace Independent Publishing Platform, 2015), Location 89.

[6] Quoted in Taber, *A Toast to Bargain Wines*, 15.

for the Chinese wine industry? How good is Chinese wine? And how good can it be?

As stated, there are more than seven hundred wineries in China today. Although it is a little bit of an oversimplification, the vast majority of the wineries fit neatly into one of two categories: the larger established producers who churn out mostly plonk to meet the growing demand for inexpensive wine and the newer wineries that try to cater to the tastes of the wealthy Chinese with money to spend on luxury goods like fine wine. In the words of wine guru Karen MacNeil—who has "won every major wine award in the English language" and is the author of *The Wine Bible*—"The cheap wines from the very large producers have mostly verged on dismal." However, this should not be considered a blanket statement regarding every wine from large producers. Also, she has positive things to say about the level of wine produced by "cutting-edge wineries" which she finds "far better." How good are these wines? MacNeil asserts: "Some of these wines are so good they could easily pass for a California or Bordeaux wine in a blind tasting." And these wines command huge sums of money. For example Chateau Hansen, which is located in Inner Mongolia, released their Red Camel cabernet sauvignon for a shade under $700 per bottle.[7]

---

[7] Karen MacNeil, *The Wine Bible*, Revised Second Edition (New York: Workman Publishing Co, 2015), 910.

CHAPTER II

A Brief History of China While Tracing the Origins of Wine Consumption

The country is quite varied in both demography and topography. China has long been shrouded in mystery for the West. In fact, the name China is an invention of the Western world. A constant theme in Western historical accounts is the homogenization of various cultures into what is modern day China. Many visitors and early historians erroneously lumped China into one culture and topography, but there is a great diversity in both.

When considering the development of China, it is important to understand that we are not discussing the triumph of a single group of "Chinese People," but rather the emergence of an amalgam of many varied cultures. Therefore, the history of what we have come to know as China is not of a single people, but of competing ethnic groups that came together. Eventually, a modern nation-state developed through centuries of war and other struggles in the face of subjugation by foreigners, such as the Mongols and Manchurians. But for those with a profound interest in the development of European grape wines in

China, we must examine the European contact with China, a relatively recent chapter in the rich and glorious history of what we now have come to call China. To understand the development of present day culture and ethnicity in China, first a brief review of the changing dynasties is essential.

Wine in China BCE

Ritualistic wine drinking, governed by specific rules, has a history that stretches back thousands of years. Rudimentary wine vessels made of pottery have been traced back to the Neolithic Period (10,000-4,000 BCE). Archaeologists discovered a bronze wine-holding vessel called a Jue in the ruins of a culture during the late Xia Dynasty; it is estimated to be more than 3,500 years old.[8]

One of the most colorful stories of wine heritage in China was that of Shao Kang, who became an important ruler during the Xia Dynasty (1989-1558 BCE). His father was killed before he was born, and he made it his mission to find the men responsible. He spent his adolescence working for his grandfather, King Qi, tending to food and affairs of hospitality. He allegedly noticed a peculiar fragrance wafting up from a grain that he had stowed in the hollow of a tree and from this deduced the alcoholic properties. When he grew up, he changed his name to Du Kang for unknown reasons and executed the man responsible for his father's murder. He eventually became king and

---

[8] Zhengping Li, *Chinese Wine: Universe in a Bottle*, Cultural China Series (New York: Cambridge University Press, 2011), 61.

spent much of his reign perfecting his winemaking technique. He became so skilled that it was said, "One bout of Du Kang's fine wine can make you drunk for three years." He solidified his legend as the father of winemaking and in the words of Li Zhengping, "His name is synonymous with good wine."[9]

Also, wine was used by many Chinese cultures as an aspect of religious sacrifice. Early records of the Western Zhou Dynasty (1046-771 BCE) show participants used fragrant wines along with other more common wines in large quantities during sacrificial ceremonies. It is estimated that more than one hundred fifty liters of wine could be used in one sacrifice. The instruments used were particular and lavish, including ladles fashioned from solid jade. Just as specific were the rules of conduct for the participants that included scattering wine on the ground to summon the spirits. Once the apparitions were thought to be among the people, they sacrificed animals including: swine, sheep, and cows. Participants would then drink wine and at the proper time begin eating food. It developed into a scene of exquisite wine-fueled revelry, but never strayed from the sacred ritualistic underpinnings. As Chinese wine researcher Li Zhenping asserts, "In sacrificial rituals like this, wine was not only the catalyst in making contact with the spirits, it also permeated the whole interchange between the world of the spirits and the world of living men."[10]

---

[9] Li, *Chinese Wine*, 14-15.

[10] Li, *Chinese Wine*, 20-22.

The Significance of the Han Dynasty

The Han was a single ethnic group that had a profound influence in shaping the culture of China. The Han ruled for several centuries (206 BCE-220 CE), leaving an indelible mark on Chinese culture. But losing power to a series of other regimes, many of which were considered foreigners, caused great distress for the Han, not to mention various other ethnic groups that were subjugated by foreign conquerors. This is an important point for those considering Chinese history and how it was recorded. For as esteemed Chinese professor and author, WJF Jenner, observed: "History as it is written in China makes it very hard even to consider the possibility that significant numbers of the subjects of Chinese regimes have refused to think of themselves as Chinese or accept the legitimacy of any Chinese rule over them and their territory."[11]

In spite of the long-standing tradition of rice wines and the fruit variations of alcoholic beverages, the grape-wine history in China continued to move forward throughout the centuries. The appearance of grape-wine production may be traced to its beginning with the Han culture.

Sima Qian (145?-90? BCE) was the grand historian for Emperor Wu, the leader who elevated the Han Dynasty to its apogee. Qian followed in the footsteps of his father, Sima Tan, who held the same

---

[11] W. J. F. Jenner, *The Tyranny of History: The Roots of China's Crisis*, Penguin History (London ; New York: Penguin Books, 1992).

position of historian as his father. Both father and son played vital roles in Chinese courts, recording the past and studying historiography. Although court historians had been a fixture in Chinese courts for a millennium, many of their records were destroyed in the frequent warfares that eventually produced the Han Dynasty. The Qin Dynasty, which preceded the Han Dynasty, further depleted historical records during their "burning of the books." This made Sima's job difficult in his time and his acclaimed work vital for posterity. He filled in what was then already ancient history to the best of his ability with the scant records that remained. He deftly recorded the recent history of especially important events as the Qin Dynasty emerged and the subsequent rise of the Han. His historical accounts won the admiration of scholars in Korea and Japan and eventually the west. To many, he is known as the father of Chinese historiography.[12]

Sima Qian's magnum opus, *The Records of the Grand Historian*, was begun by his father and the elder Sima implored his son to complete his work as his last dying wish. The younger Sima made the completion of this work his focus and his desire to finish faced the ultimate test because he found himself on the receiving end of Emperor Wu's fiery temper. For his role in a sticky internal affair that Wu sought fit to meet with severe punishment, Sima was sentenced to castration and jailed. A man of his stature would have the customary option of taking his own life and saving face while avoiding the pain and humiliation of

---

[12] Qian Sima, *Records of the Grand Historian: Han Dynasty I*, trans. Burton Watson, Rev. ed, Records of Civilization 65 (Hong Kong: Columbia Univ. Press Book, 1993), xv-xvii.

the decree. However, he elected to fulfill his vow to his father and suffer the excruciating consequences so that he could complete the work that enriched the lives of countless students of history and opened the portal to his own immortality.[13]

He had a keen eye for detail, rendering people and customs vividly in seemingly three-dimensional accounts. Among the topics he touched upon were some of the earliest accounts of the elaborate wine rituals that have pervaded Chinese history. He described a scene when the King of the Han had finally vanquished the Qin and was poised to receive the title "Supreme Emperor" at a lavish ceremony. Banners were unfurled and guards stood brandishing gleaming weaponry. When the emperor entered, the din drew to a silence as he surveyed the guests from his litter. There were hundreds of guests from powerful nobles to lowly officials and "every one trembled with awe and reverence."[14]

When the ceremony ended, the wine ritual began. All of his subjects bowed until the monarch allowed them to rise, according to their rank, and enjoy a cup of wine, toasting his reign. Nine times the vessel was passed. Those who did not perform the ritual properly were banished from the hall. Although they had copious servings of wine, heeding the example made of their colleagues, there was no rowdy behavior from those who remained. While raising a cup, the jubilant emperor exclaimed, "Today for the first time I realize how exalted a thing it is to be emperor!"[15]

---

[13] Ibid.

[14] Ibid, 243.

[15] Ibid, 243-244.

This colorful tale shows that there is a deep cultural heritage of ritualistic drinking. Although the drink of choice was generally rice wine or some combination of grains, which could occasionally include grapes, the important part is the precedent. It is important to consider that the significant rise in wine consumption in modern times did not occur in a vacuum. Rather, it grew from a deep history of alcohol consumption in various iterations. When viewed through the prism of the long history of ritualistic drinking and the particular tastes of the Chinese people, perhaps the modern grape wine industry can be seen as an inevitability rather than an anomaly. Qian's story is an illustration that has bearing on today's wine culture. The vital role of wine in a ceremony indicates it was a symbol of status. We will later see how gift giving has an important role when it comes to social status.

It is important to emphasize that the wine consumed by the emperor in Sima Qian's colorful tale was most likely not exclusively made of grapes. In general, alcoholic concoctions were often referred to broadly as "wine" whether they were derived from sorghum, rice, honey, grapes, or some combination. Until the T'ang dynasty, any sort of wine exclusively made from grapes was extremely rare. Pinpointing the exact date that winemaking was invented in China is impossible. However, legends of the invention of winemaking abound.

The Rise of Grape Wine During the T'ang Dynasty

The T'ang Dynasty (618-907) was a golden era where art and civil society flourished. Buddhism found its way to China and melded with traditional Chinese philosophies to initiate an era of spiritual blossoming. This was the time when the ideographic writing system was put to standard use, resulting in the emergence of elegant calligraphy and eloquent poetry. This was the era when an authentically Chinese culture emerged and burgeoned. The T'ang Dynasty is important because this is the first time we see grape wine emerging as a minor theme in the art and literature of China.

Due to discoveries of wine being first depicted in T'ang literature, it is assumed that grape wine consumption seems to be rooted in the early T'ang Dynasty. In fact, *The Fragrant Nine Crooked Stream* is a popular tale from the tradition of The Eight Immortals of Taoism, which is traced back to the T'ang dynasty. In this tale, the popular immortal named Ti Kuai Li has a great desire to try the wine produced by a man called the Farm Father who resides near the Nine Crooked Stream in Bohea (apparently near Bohea hills in the present-day province of Fujian). In the story, the Farm Father makes a wine so good that even the gods are envious, and the hero of the story Ti Kuai Li is so fond of the wine that it causes him to make a ruckus in heaven so calamitous that he ends up cracking the pot that the wine is held in, and it flows into the stream so: "The wine still trickles into the waters of the Nine Crooked Stream to this day and this is why the air in Bohea is so fragrant." During the story, Ti Kuai Li asks the Farm Father why his wine is so divine, and he replies: "I grow vines close to the rice fields, I take water from the Nine Crooked Stream..." To which Ti Kuai Li excitedly replies: "It is the land and water of Bohea that gives it its unique taste. I hope this land never fails to yield such pleasing fruits."[16]

This story is significant because it most likely refers to grape wine as he mentions "vines" and "fruits", showing that by the early T'ang, grape wine was not only becoming known, but its praises were becoming ingrained in the folklore that would be passed down throughout the centuries. It becomes more significant when one considers this bit of verse, written in the eighth century by Li Ch'i, which describes the plight of the early T'ang warriors who guarded the empire at the frontier against those peoples who were considered barbarian and a threat to the empire:

Yellow clouds at Goose Gate Canton—
Where sun sets behind wind and sand;
A thousand horsemen in black sable furs—
All styled "Boys of the Feather Forest."
Gold clarinets blow through boreal snow,

---

[16] Man-Ho Kwok and Joanne O'Brien, eds., *The Eight Immortals of Taoism: Legends and Fables of Popular Taoism* (New York, N.Y., U.S.A: Meridian, 1991), 95-97.

Iron horses neigh by clouded waters:

Under the tents they are drinking the grape—

And this is the very inch-big heart of their lives.[17]

This verse suggests that grape wine was an integral part of the existence of these hardened warriors. Moreover, it shows that the consumption of grape wine was not reserved only for royalty, but consumed by other members of the empire. Wine was not only used to slake the thirst of warriors at the edge of the empire, but it was popular in the taverns and bordellos in grand cities such as Ch'ang-an where a sly bar-owner could boost his profits by hiring an exotic beauty from the West and have her pour expensive wine. This phenomenon was captured in the meter of poet Li Po,[18] who was a colorful character and a famous advocate of wine consumption. Li was known to imbibe large quantities of wine which led to his unfortunate, yet rather poetic, death. As the story goes, Li became so enamored with the reflection of the full moon in a river that he tried to embrace it and drowned:[19]

The zither plays "The Green Paulownias at Dragon Gate,"

The lovely wine, in its pot of jade, is as clear as the sky.

As I press against the strings, and brush across the studs, I'll drink with you, milord;

---

[17] Edward H. Schafer, *The Golden Peaches of Samarkand: A Study of T'ang Exotics* (Berkeley, Calif.: Univ. of California Press, 1963), 107-108.

[18] Note that he is sometimes also referred to as "Li Bai" in China.

[19] Alexis Lichine and William Fifield, *Alexis Lichine's New Encyclopedia of Wines & Spirits*, 5th ed., rev (New York: Knopf, 1987), 180.

"Vermilion will seem to be prase-green" when our faces begin to redden.

That Western houri with features like a flower—

She stands by the wine-warmer, and laughs with the breath of spring

Laughs with the breath of spring,

Dances in a dress of gauze!

"Will you be going somewhere, milord, *now*, before you are drunk?"[20]

The Manchus

The Manchus, whose dynastic period is referred to as the Qing Dynasty (1644-1912), not only subjugated the Han Chinese, but humiliated them by forcing them to adopt their peculiar hairstyle that involved shaving the front of their craniums and also adopting their unorthodox style of dress. Although the Han had been conquered by other ethnic groups besides the Manchus, it is important to remember that they are the ethnic group that make up the vast majority of China's population and have remained an important cultural force in China throughout its history. Nevertheless, while the Manchus were busy trying to consolidate power and quash dissent in China, they had to contend with the imperial ambitions of burgeoning European powers, namely France and England. As Jenner reminds us, "Like any other state, China is a figment of the imagination, of many imaginations. There is no inherent necessity determining the borders of the present

---

[20] Schafer, *The Golden Peaches of Samarkand*, 21.

Chinese state. Those borders are more the product of the relative strengths of empires, Manchu and European, in the late nineteenth and early twentieth centuries than anything else."[21]

China in the 1800s

The British brutally opened China to trade with the West and became obsessed with Chinese tea. Britain's imports from China were far outpacing the goods that were being sent in the opposite direction. In an effort to balance the trade deficit, the British began selling large blocks of opium to Chinese traders with damaging effects on the society. With their society crumbling and tons of silver leaving for England, the Chinese had had enough. Tensions led to the First Opium War (1839-1842), which ended with the Chinese giving major concessions to England after being forced to sign an embarrassingly lopsided treaty.

In the 1850s and 1860s China was devastated by interior rebellions and renewed conflicts with both France and England. After decades of foreign intervention by the European imperial powers and the Manchus, who themselves were also considered foreign usurpers, China drew itself in, hoping to regain sovereignty, and briefly attempted a democratic government.

---

[21] Jenner, *The Tyranny of History*, 2.

China in the 1900s

The period of the Republic of China (1911-1949) was marred by internal strife and a war with the Japanese. In 1949, Mao Zedong established the People's Republic of China and the communist vision of Mao would continue until his death in 1976. Mao was succeeded by Deng Xiaoping who instituted a radical economic vision for China that embraced aspects of market economics. Although his economic vision is different than Mao's, he continued the totalitarianism that marks the People's Republic of China, which continues today. One of the most important developments which still drives the economy and consequently affects the wine industry is the Five Year Plans.

China's Five Year Plans were instated for social and economic development. They would outline initiatives that if utilized would allow for rapid development. This was the focus of Mao Zedong when he introduced the first in 1953. The plans were composed of various aspects of development through collectivized agriculture and collections of artisans along with other aspects based upon the Soviet economic model. The Five Year Plans became a central part of the PRC's continued development of the Chinese economy. Today we are in the thirteenth Five Year Plan which spans 2016-2020.

CHAPTER III

The Turn to Spirits and Other Types of Alcohol in China

Wines derived from grapes fell out of favor in China sometime during the latter part of the T'ang Dynasty, in conjunction with a rise in alcoholic beverages derived from grains such as sorghum and millet. Sorghum formed the base of baijiu, a fiery spirit that has been consumed in China for millennia and remains the utmost popular spirit worldwide in terms of consumption. China is the largest spirits market in the world.[22]

Historically, the most popular liquor in China is referred to as *baijiu*, which has been produced in China for millennia. However, the term *baijiu* can be confusing because it is a general term that is approximately translated as "white alcohol," "white liquor," and in some cases "schnapps." It is important to note that *jiu* is generally translated as "alcohol." So grape wine, for example, is often referred to

---

[22] "Hong Kong's Wine Market with Prospects Until 2017" (*Vinexpo Asia-Pacific*, May 2014), http://studylib.net/doc/7694851/hong-kong-s-wine-market-with-prospects-until-2017--source.

as *putao-jiu*. Under the umbrella term baijiu, there are many variations which are sometimes grouped in two categories: flavored and unflavored.

Perhaps the most notable form of *baijiu* is *Maotai*, a strong and rich spirit that is usually between 100 and 110 proof. Another flavored form is Shuijingfang which is a precursor to *Maotai*. *Shuijingfang* liquor's roots date back five thousand years, in a system that used particular microbes to create what beverage scholar Li Zhengping refers to as a spirit with "smooth texture, unique aroma, elegant flavor and a pleasant lingering aftertaste."[23]

But China's earliest preferred alcoholic beverages were generally not strong liquors, but sweeter drinks. The many early palates were also attuned to sweeter spirits made from fruits like lychee. With this flavor preference of the times, there was also a rise in consumption of plum wine, still popular in China today. With a few notable exceptions, these beverages became the alcoholic beverages of choice for many in China. Until the final two decades of the twentieth century, with a few notable exceptions, grape wine was rarely consumed in China. In fact, the World Health Organization estimated that wine derived from grapes accounted for less than one percent of all alcohol consumed in the country in 1970.[24]

---

[23] Li, *Chinese Wine*, 34-44.

[24] MacNeil, *The Wine Bible*, 908-909.

Other Types of "Wine" Consumed in China

As mentioned before, the term "wine" in China has a very different meaning than in the West. In the West, wine is almost exclusively made with *Vitis vinifera* and contains nothing but grapes. However, in China there is a long-standing tradition of drinking rice wine and wine made of other fruits (most notably plum wine), which predates the use of grapes in making wine. Therefore, the term wine is used widely to describe various alcoholic beverages. The distinction between what the West would refer to as wine from everything else is a relatively new phenomenon in China.

Rice wine (also referred to as "yellow wine") is the traditional "wine" consumed in China. Some of the most popular wines are: Shaoxing Yellow Wine, Jimo Old Wine (also called *laojiu*), and Red Ferment Wine which uses mold that grows on polished round rice. So, it is interesting to ponder why rice wine has been so ubiquitous in China for millenia, while grape wine is only recently coming into fashion. This interesting observation by Li Zhengping may offer an important insight into why rice wine, which once dominated Chinese palates, is now being supplanted by grape wine: "Grape wine is easier to produce than rice wine. However, as grapes are seasonal and cannot retain their freshness for long compared to grain, grape wine-making technology was not adopted extensively in ancient China."[25]

---

[25] Li, *Chinese Wine*, 24-29.

Vitis Vinifera in China

The introduction of *Vitis vinifera* can be traced back to the early Han Dynasty. Although China has several native grape varieties that can be used to produce wine, *Vitis vinifera* was an import. When Chang Chien, a general returning to China from a journey to Fergana in 128 BCE, reported with amazement how the affluent members of Fergana stored thousands of gallons of wine for dozens of years without spoilage, he triumphantly presented the seeds which were then planted near the imperial palace, setting a precedent for future cultivation. The advancement of the Silk Road enabled the proliferation of other wine grape varieties in China. Many foreigners had since mentioned the proliferation of vines that produced wine grapes. In the thirteenth century, Marco Polo noted, "In Shanxi province grew many excellent vines, supplying a great deal of wine, and in all Cathay this is the only place where wine is produced. It is carried hence all over the country."[26]

Grapes were not an important fruit, and for centuries after Chang Chien brought the first *Vitis vinifera* to China the wine produced from fermented grapes was rarely consumed. However, it is important to note that China has many other varieties of wine and table grapes which are either native or predate the arrival of *Vitis vinifera*. Not until the T'ang Dynasty pushed west into the lands that make up modern Turkey and Iran did wine start to become known to larger portions of

---

[26] Hugh Johnson, *Vintage: The Story of Wine* (New York: Simon and Schuster, 1989), 20-21.

the population. Also, table grapes were consumed along with raisins, but not in large quantities. Most of the wine produced was reserved for special occasions, a usage that is most closely reflected in the way Champagne is consumed in the West today. Even powerful emperors regarded wine as an exotic novelty. In the ninth century, Emperor Mu Tsung reflected after a sip of grape wine, "When I drink this, I am instantly conscious of harmony suffusing my four limbs—it is the true 'Princeling of Grand Tranquility'!" This was perhaps evoking the moniker of the great sage Lao Tzu, while also suggesting the idea, represented by Dionysus in Greek Mythology and Bacchus in Rome, that wine is deeply entwined with the divine.[27]

Wine was also an ingredient in various concoctions used in Chinese medicine. These nostrums seemed to emerge during the T'ang Dynasty. If a man found himself bleeding without any obvious reason, he was instructed to consume ashes from hair and fingernail clippings soaked in wine.[28] If impotence was the issue, it was suggested that a man could be cured by consuming a dried phallus of a White Horse along with honey in wine.[29]

Although the accompaniments of the wine may seem bizarre by modern measures, it is not strange to see wine as a substance beneficial to one's health. The precedent for wine's salubrious potential has its

---

[27] Schafer, *The Golden Peaches of Samarkand*, 180-181.

[28] Ibid, 194.

[29] Ibid, 180-181.

roots in the T'ang Dynasty. The healthful properties of wine played a key role in the expansion of the industry in Modern China.

Besides the cultural ramifications of developing grape wines in China, the topography and climate also played a role in its development. China is the fourth largest nation in the world, geographically; and within the 3.7 million square miles that comprise the nation, there is nearly every kind of topography and climate on Earth. However, the weather tends toward the extreme in ways that are not conducive to cultivating wine grapes. This situation is rectified by the massive tractable labor that overcomes the extreme difficulties that the climate presents. In the Ningxia Hui Autonomous Region and Inner Mongolia, the vines must withstand extreme drops in temperature to -20 degrees Fahrenheit. The necessity of dealing with these extremes has birthed the solutions of what is known as "deep-ditch cultivation." The local farmers dig trenches three to five feet in the ground and then plant the vines within. As the plants mature the agriculturalists add more dirt which builds up the mass of soil and the result is that all of the newest and most vulnerable roots are covered and thusly protected. Moreover, the most mature roots are burrowing deeper into the soil and protecting themselves from the extreme cold.[30]

Frigid winds that blow down from Siberia make the winters too cold for *Vitis vinifera* to survive in many parts of northern China where the species now thrives. New viticultural procedures, large pools of labor, and sheer determination have transformed the fate of

---

[30] MacNeil, *The Wine Bible*, 911.

the sought-after wine-producing grapes. This explains why it took until modern times for *Vitis vinifera* to take root in China and begin to produce desirable wines.[31]

As a result of the climate, there are cold weather grapes that are grown in China that have done well in places like Georgia (Republic) and Russia including rkatsiteli and saperavi. However, red varieties dominate the viticulture which is natural, given the Chinese passion for red wine. This includes: cabernet sauvignon, cabernet franc, syrah, pinot noir, merlot, and a varietal that is referred to as cabernet gernischt. Interestingly, DNA testing has revealed that cabernet gernischt is exactly the same as carménère, a grape that was originally planted in the Bordeaux region of France and has done exceedingly well in South America. As we shall later see, Bordeaux wines, particularly reds, are valued most highly in China. In Bordeaux, these wines are always blended from several grape varieties depending on conditions as the blends may change from year to year. This tradition is certainly reflected in the grapes cultivated for Chinese wines.[32]

---

[31] Mustacich, *Thirsty Dragon*, 65.

[32] MacNeil, *The Wine Bible*, 912.

CHAPTER IV

Factors That Affected the Rise in Consumption and Production of Grape Wine in China

Emperor Kangxi Sets a Precedent for Wine in Modern China

Emperor Kangxi (1654-1722) had perhaps the most significant case of diarrhea in wine history early on in his reign. The disease persisted until a European missionary suggested that he drink a little grape wine to cure his ailment.[33] At first, the emperor was wary, but desperate for a cure, he followed the instructions. At the missionary's behest, he continued to drink a little wine each day until he was cured. He was amazed at the healing quality of the wine that he quickly grew to enjoy. He developed a passion for wine for the rest of his life,

---

[33] Although the identity of the missionary who provided the wine for Kangxi is not certain, there were numerous Jesuit missionaries who held important positions in his court. Therefore, the missionary was most likely a Jesuit.

continuing to have a little wine every day, which was a habit formed during his ailment. The moment is considered the first "official" introduction of European wine to China since the consumption of wine derived from European grapes (*Vitis Vinifera*) had not been consumed by the Emperor before. His habit of drinking this wine can be traced back as a seminal moment in the history of European wine consumption and cultivation in China.[34]

Emperor Kangxi reigned for sixty-one years before his death in 1722. During this long reign, he had time to address a number of social issues, but he was at his core a tinkerer who had a passion for grape wine. He is credited with testing numerous varieties of wine grapes in many different locales within his kingdom in hopes of finding new and exciting ways to cultivate grapes and enjoy wine. He is considered to be one of China's greatest emperors and perhaps his egalitarian approach to agriculture contributed to his legacy. As he once famously asserted: "I would rather procure for my subjects a novel kind of fruit or grain, than build a hundred porcelain kilns."[35]

No other ruler during the Qing Dynasty (1616-1911) shared Kangxi's passion for grape cultivation. In fact, industrial cultivation of wine in China did not begin until 1892 when businessman Chang Bishi established the Changyu Wine Production Company in the Shandong Province. The Changyu Wine Production Company was started with

---

[34] Li, *Chinese Wine*, 134.

[35] Johnson, *Vintage.*, 20-21.

three million tael of silver[36] as seed money. That money was used to bring in state-of-the-art equipment from Europe and wine specialists from around the world. Changyu began producing brandy along with red and white wine in the first serious modern endeavor to make world class wine in China. The production of great wine was built upon a foundation philosophy of mixing Western and Chinese techniques to produce extraordinary wine. The company began with high hopes, which is evident from the name *Changyu* which comes from Chang Bishi's surname, Chang. The word *Yu* is the Chinese word for "prosperity." In pursuit of lasting prosperity, Chang built in 1905 a modern wine cellar that was the biggest in all of Asia at the time. The winery did not formally open until 1914. But it had an auspicious start, capturing four gold medals at the Panama Pacific International Exposition in 1915.[37]

About one hundred years later, a plucky British businessman named Chris Ruffle would add an interesting new chapter to this history in the present day when he founded his Treaty Port Vineyards in Shandong, bottling his first vintage in 2010. His unique journey is chronicled in his book, *A Decent Bottle of Wine in China,* which is not only entertaining, but also instructive. Evident from Ruffle's account, the wine industry has changed drastically since Chang Bishi bottled his first wine nearly a century earlier. We will explore those changes in depth in subsequent chapters.

---

[36] A tael of silver is approximately 1.3 ounces of silver. So this amount was nearly four million ounces of silver which would be worth approximately $68 million today.

[37] Li, *Chinese Wine*, 51-55.

Wine in Communist China

In 1949, soon after the communist party took power in China, Changyu was nationalized and focused on making brandy, to the delight of the communist party's senior leaders.[38] Under communist rule, the consumption of baijiu among other spirits and beer dominated the Chinese alcohol industry. Commonly, tipplers at lavish Chinese banquets, often thrown by a member of the communist party, were encouraged to "*Gan bei*" which roughly translates to empty the glass. In America, there are other related phrases such as "bottoms up." Tony Stavely, professor emeritus at Keene State College and oenophile who has spent time in China, recalls speaking with a U.S. diplomat who served in Taiwan. He taught Stavely that at a proper Chinese banquet, a toast must be made by someone who wants a sip of wine, and then all at the table must raise a glass and sip also. The consumption of alcohol in China is often done by adherence to social rules garnered from old traditions. These traditions have made for some interesting situations for foreigners who are newly initiated into the drinking culture and perhaps no drinking tale is more colorful and significant than that of Richard Nixon's visit.

In the winter of 1972, president Richard Nixon sat at a lavish dinner held in Beijing's Great Hall of the People, surrounded by many of China's elite. This occasion was the eve of a momentous change in geopolitics. Nixon was encouraged by Zhou Enlai, Mao's number one

---

[38] Taber, *A Toast to Bargain Wines*, 145.

man, to *gan bei* the powerful *baijiu* in his cup. Instead, Nixon timidly sipped the fiery booze, walking a fine line of not insulting his hosts, while not getting too plastered to continue his negotiations. Nixon's caginess proved fruitful for the United States and the Chinese wine industry, eventually opening China up to the West. But soon Chinese politics was headed for more major adjustments. As Chairman Mao's days were numbered, the party began to drift in a different direction.[39]

The most significant change in the economic structure of the People's Republic of China (PRC) came with the emergence of Deng Xiaoping after the death of Chairman Mao in 1976. Deng drastically changed the Chinese communist orthodoxy by moving from a command economy to what was referred to as "Socialism with Chinese Characteristics." Deng rationalized this move with this famous analogy: "It doesn't matter if a cat is black or white, so long as it catches mice." As time wore on, China's financial success was seen as fueling a rise in alcohol consumption. The grains used to make certain liquors were produced on a larger scale, making them cheaper and more available. Also, more people had disposable income to purchase powerful liquor, namely *baijiu*. The prevailing solution in the party was that the grains that were once used to produce hard liquor could be better utilized as fodder for animals and to feed the masses of starving Chinese who did not have the same opportunities as those with close ties to the ruling government. This created a demand for something to fill the void.[40]

---

[39] Ibid, 144.

[40] Ibid, 144-145.

Deng had an ambitious plan to double the nation's GDP during the 1980s. Although Chinese economy saw unprecedented growth under Deng, the party was still grappling with starvation and malnourishment as it strained to feed its rapidly growing population. This made the expensive *baijiu* that was still being consumed by the leadership (sometimes to the point of notable inebriation) a conspicuously frivolous way to use grains that could feed their starving countrymen. Unlike sorghum, rice and other grains used for *baijiu*, grapes could be grown in a wide array of territories, even in places where the soil and other vital conditions were not hospitable to growing grains used in *baijiu*.[41]

Li Peng's Proclamation is the Spark that Ignites the Wine Industry

All of these currents flowed together, coming to a head at an extraordinary moment in 1996. Li Peng, who was Premier at the time, stood before the National People's Congress in Beijing and praised red wine for its many benefits to the health of the individual and for the country. He criticized the use of *baijiu* and called for change. He solidified his position at future banquets by being careful to provide red wine which he would hold high in the air for toasts where in the past, those glasses would have been filled with *baijiu*. The pronouncement of Li combined with a wave of news pieces on the merits of red wine in

---

[41]Mustacich, *Thirsty Dragon*, 14.

maintaining and improving heath, especially cardiovascular health, made it an almost instant hit. Moreover, red is a lucky color in China, so red wine was an easy sell. The fortune of those who loved red wine in China and others who sought to profit from this growing industry had just taken a massive positive turn.[42]

The impact of Li's proclamation was timely, and the impact was widespread. To meet the growing demand, China was shipping wine in by the 22,000-liter bag. In 1996, Fernando Rovira was in charge of international sales at the Bodegas Félix Solis winery located in Spain. He recalls that the orders started rolling in from China for significant volumes of wine. "People wanted four, five containers in the first order, no sample required," he reflected.[43]

The proclamation by Li in 1996 coincided with the Ninth Five-Year-Plan approved by the National People's Congress in the same year. This plan insisted upon a dramatic increase in the quantity of grapes produced domestically and an increased production of wine. Since vineyard production was not robust enough to meet government demands, many wineries including Great Wall and Dynasty (two of the "Big Three" producers along with Changyu), imported grapes from

---

[42] Aryn Baker, "The Sweet Taste of Success," *Time*, May 16, 2005, http://content.time.com/time/subscriber/article/0,33009,1059080,00.html.

[43] Pieter Eijkhoff, *Wine in China: Its History and Contemporary Developments* (Utrecht: P. Eijkhoff : Nederlands Wijngilde, 2000), http://www.eykhoff.nl/Wine%20in%20China.pdf. Dissertation to obtain the degree Grandmaster Wine Taster of Dutch Wine Guild.

Australia, South America, Spain, and even France. The wine industry was on the rise, and so was the purchasing power of the Chinese expanding consumer class.[44]

The industry was in the midst of a viticultural gold rush and many enterprising individuals scrambled to get a piece of the action. Before Li's proclamation, there were several dozen vineyards, but that number swelled to three hundred in just a few years. In a single year, the volume of wine consumption almost tripled in China, and imports grew sixfold.[45] The wine industry was not the only aspect of the Chinese economy that was roaring.

Deng Xiaoping's economic overhaul ushered in a period of rapid industrialization and transformed the nation from a more collective structure with a state-run economy (command economy) into one of many have-nots and a small growing class of *nouveau riche*. China experienced decades of rapid economic growth. Next to the United States, China has more billionaires than any other country in the world.[46] China is fourth worldwide in the number of millionaires.[47]

---

[44] Mustacich, *Thirsty Dragon*, 87.

[45] Eijkhoff, *Wine in China*, 136.

[46] Kathleen Elkins, "There Are More Billionaires in the US than in China, Germany and India Combined," CNBC.com, May 15, 2018, https://uk.finance.yahoo.com/news/more-billionaires-us-china-germany-165900809.html.

[47] Lovemoney Staff, "The Countries with the Most Millionaires Revealed," MSN, June 20, 2017, https://www.msn.com/en-in/news/other/the-countries-with-the-most-millionaires-revealed/ss-BBzsCIg.

Moreover, Beijing, Shanghai, and Hong Kong rank in the top ten wealthiest cities in the world.[48]

As the nation was creating an ultra-rich class, China was opening up to the rest of the globe and curiosity about the West, and its trappings soon followed. The taste for Western luxury in the form of BMWs, Gucci, and a thirst for the best of Bordeaux flourished; fine wine became a symbol of success for many. The story about a rising class of industrial entrepreneurs is one that is pertinent to the development of a prosperous wine industry. The developing role of wine as something to enjoy, to learn about, and as a way to show off one's status in China is pivotal in explaining its current popularity. Moreover, it was used as a means to flatter and in some cases bribe. Wine is an interesting prism through which to view China's economic ascent and their emergence on the world stage as a player in many key markets.[49]

The 1855 Classification in Bordeaux

In order to understand the prestige and desire to purchase Bordeaux in China, a review of its historical development is necessary. The French term *terroir* is derived from the Latin word *terre* which means "land." Terroir refers to a combination of environmental factors that give a

---

[48] Amarendra Bhushan Dhiraj, "World's 15 Richest Cities In 2017: New York, London, And Tokyo, Tops List," *CEOWORLD Magazine* (blog), February 12, 2018, http://ceoworld.biz/2018/02/12/worlds-15-richest-cities-in-2017-new-york-london-and-tokyo-tops-list/.

[49] MacNeil, *The Wine Bible*, 909.

crop specific characteristics. The main factors are geomorphology, climate, soil type and surrounding vegetation. Terroir is the basis for the French appellation d'origine controlee (AOC) laws which grant certain distinctions to wine, cheese, and other agricultural products based upon their geographical origin. One of the most popular examples of this is that sparkling white wine derived from the Champagne region in France is the only sparkling white wine that can be referred to as Champagne. The AOC system is the basis for appellation (the geographic region a wine is produced in). Regulation of wines is not only in practice in France, but around the world, with most European countries having some sort of classification.

Just as Champagne is synonymous with world-class sparkling white wine, Bordeaux is an appellation of what many consider to be the best red wine in the world, the vast majority of which are blends. Bordeaux does things differently than many other premier wine producing regions, which has helped to set it on a pedestal as the best in the mind of novices and well-educated aficionados. One of the most important aspects of Bordeaux's sustained success is the 1855 Classification. It is important to note here that although the concept of the AOC has roots in the fifteenth century, it did not come about until 1935 with the inception of the *Comité National des appellations d'origine* (CNAO), which was given complete authority over the matters that relate to wine quality. In 1936, the initial AOC laws were passed. By 1937, most of the major regions including Bordeaux, Rhone, and Burgundy had established their first set of AOC regulations. As we shall see, the 1855

Bordeaux Classification was an important part of this process, and it would even play a key role in the modern Chinese wine market.

How 1855 Distinguished Bordeaux

In 1855, the Universal Exhibition in Paris showcased exciting goods for visitors from around the world. Wine was an important part of the Universal Exhibition and several regions put their best on display, including Champagne and Burgundy. Winemakers in Bordeaux knew they had something special and did not want to be outshone by their famous colleagues in regions like Champagne. In this era, wine was purchased by wholesale wine sellers called *négociants* who bought the wine in bulk from the producers and then bottled and labelled it before bringing the wine to market. *Négociants* would routinely acquire wines from multiple vineyards and blend them themselves after it had been expertly aged. This meant that the name of the *négociant* on the bottle was generally of more importance than that of the châteaux (the plural of château, which roughly translates to "manor house" and in this case refers to the estates that produced the wine). However, certain estates became known for the exceptional quality of their wines regardless of which *négociant* distributed their wine. These were referred to as "château" wines. In the case of 1855, there were far too many wines for each to be represented individually. All of the *négociants* and châteaux had a stake in the game, each with their own particular incentives. So, how could they represent the entirety of Bordeaux properly without unfairly slighting individual producers, while not putting the wine in the same identical bottle which would have the effect of making Bordeaux wine appear generic? This quandary had to be resolved in the most efficient way, providing the fairest resolution for each constituent.[50]

They decided to display the wine with individual bottles bearing the name of the owner along with the corresponding chateau. Each was placed on an enlarged map of the Bordeaux region, so revelers at the exhibition could get a sense of the region. Sixty wines were then ranked in a hierarchical system of five *crus* (growths) with the best wines placed in the category of *Premier Crus* (First Growths), then Second Growths, Third Growths, Fourth Growths, and then Fifth Growths (the lowest distinction within the 1855 system). Each growth was presented with a range of prices marking their particular classifications.[51]

No one involved in the 1855 Classification expected it to last, for it was simply an expedient way to solve a problem. Interestingly, the system was so popular that it became a basis for judging the region ever since its inception. In fact, the only change in the system until 1973 was adding Château Cantemerle to the Fifth Growths. In 1973, the final change came when Château Mouton Rothschild was elevated to a First Growth along with the other elites: Château Haut-Brion, Château Latour, Château Margaux, and the illustrious Château Lafite. Although the châteaux that were left out of the system chafed under the weight of

---

[50] Mustacich, *Thirsty Dragon*, 6-7.

[51] Ibid, 7-8.

a system that did not appreciate their efforts as much as some of their neighbors, the system was a resounding success. It created a mystique around wines from the Bordeaux region that elevated it to a unique position in the eyes of wine lovers worldwide for generations. But it should be stressed that although the 1855 classification helped elevate the popularity of the wine because it is easy to follow, Bordeaux has risen to prominence because the region has historically produced some of the best wine in the world. It later had a profound influence on the Chinese wine market.[52]

Status and "Face" in Chinese Culture

To understand the profound impact of the 1855 Classification on China, one must have an understanding of "face" in China. Face is a sociological concept that describes one's prestige in certain social situations—something that is of great social importance in China. This concept can be explained for our purposes with a better understanding of the cultural mores expressed as *gei mianzi* and *liu mianzi*. *Mianzi* is a noun which roughly translates to "respect." *Gei mianzi* is a verb which refers to gaining social validation (or status) from displaying respect to someone. *Gei mianzi* was often practiced by giving a present to someone that was suitable for their social standing. It became common for high ranking officials to receive expensive watches, fine wine, and other gifts from those seeking favors. *Liu mianzi* honor can be won by

---

[52] Ibid, 8.

the avoidance of making mistakes, such as a faux pas. Therefore, the 1855 Classification fit China perfectly because it was a simple way to ensure that the gift giver was offering a bona fide present that would ensure both *gei mianzi* and *liu mianzi*. These concepts must be considered within the context of the rapid industrialization under the Chinese Communist Party, where the right gift can grease the wheels for a lucrative government contract, for example. Such venality came to a head in 2012 and caused the government to launch an anti-corruption campaign which we will examine in depth later.[53]

How the 1855 Classification Relates to the Wine Industry in China

Savvy importers like Thomas Yip, who founded the Hong Kong-based TOPSY TRADING COMPANY LTD. in 1982, understood that the 1855 Classification made Bordeaux a perfect choice for fine wine in China. Yip was the most successful importer at the vanguard of China's growing interest in Bordeaux. They were able to sell a small volume of wines from the higher crus, which were set by the 1855 Classification, to members of the growing pool of wealthy Chinese. However, the market quickly changed after Li Peng's 1996 ordination of red wine as the preferred alcoholic drink in China. This spike in red wine consumption occurred in both Hong Kong and mainland China.

---

[53] Ibid, 8.

People with means were ordering red wine while out to dinner or singing karaoke. The wine was not usually from Bordeaux; often it was inexpensive and domestically produced. Not being attuned to the taste, the wine was often mixed with lemonade or soda to make it easier to drink. This was a practice that continued in China for a long time, and it was rumored that not only table wine was being mixed with cola, but expensive Bordeaux as well. However, it is important to note that with time and education the tastes of the Chinese public is changing, and by and large they are much more savvy about the wine they consume and continue to have an unquenchable thirst for wine education.[54]

Therefore, with all the interest and growth in red wine following Li Peng's 1996 proclamation about red wine, it was a key moment in the modern history of wine in China and certainly had a significant positive impact on consumption. In 1995, China had about 240 wineries; by 1997 China had added an additional two hundred wineries. But did a simple proclamation by the Communist party change the tastes of China? Not exactly; it was just the most important moment that sat on top of a confluence of factors.[55]

Yang Lu, an award-winning Chinese sommelier, offered this valuable insight in 2014: "Wine has really only become important in China in the last ten years. But we have tea, which is probably as complex as wine. It is such a big part of our culture. For generations, for a thousand years, we have appreciated tea. This gives us a very subtle

---

[54] Ibid, 8

[55] Ibid, 56.

and sophisticated palate in terms of drinking and this has now translated into wine as it has become more popular."[56]

In *Thirsty Dragon: China's Lust for Bordeaux and the Threat to the World's Best Wines*, author Suzanne Mustacich deftly explains how Bordeaux captured the hearts and wallets of wealthy Chinese consumers. She chronicles how the Chinese thirst for Bordeaux drove the international market for the region's wine through the ceiling, in a frenzy that was nearly as unbelievable as the seventeenth century tulip craze in The Netherlands. But the market came back to Earth after the astonishing successes of the 2009 and 2010 vintages. More recently the tastes of China's elite have shifted to Burgundy, where wines from the Côte d'Or are now more popular and fetching higher prices than wines from Bordeaux. But one aspect that endures is the close relationship between China and France when it comes to fermented grapes. French wine still accounts for about half of China's wine consumption.[57]

---

[56] Will Lyons, "The People's Republic of Wine," *Wall Street Journal*, February 7, 2014, sec. Europe, https://www.wsj.com/articles/the-people8217s-republic-of-wine-1391736358.

[57] Roberto A. Ferdman, "China Now Guzzles More Red Wine than Any Other Country in the World," *Quartz* (blog), February 1, 2014, https://qz.com/172874/china-now-guzzles-more-red-wine-than-any-other-country-in-the-world/.

CHAPTER V

China's Forays into the International Wine Scene

The first formal initiation into the international wine scene came in 1979 when China sent representatives to the L'Organisation Internationale de la Vigne et du Vin (OIV).[58] The Chinese have long viewed France as the homeland of the world's greatest wine. French businessmen who make a living in wine have long considered China a land of unparalleled opportunity. The year 1980 marked the first of many joint ventures between major players in the French and Chinese wine industries with Rémy Martin signing a deal to create Dynasty Fine Wines. The name was, amusingly, taken from one of the most popular television shows at the time, bearing the same name. Rémy Martin was given a 38 percent stake in the venture with Tianjin (a municipality of about seven million people which is the closest post to Beijing) keeping the balance. One of the former Chinese executives

---

[58] The OIV is referred to as the International Organization of Vine and Wine in English. We will continue to use this name in all subsequent references. According to their website, the OIV is "an intergovernmental organization concerning itself with the scientific and technical aspects of viticulture, oenology and the vitivinicultural economy."

had this to say about the "satisfactory" deal: "Since Rémy Martin was eager to gain a firm foothold in China, and we needed to study French advanced wine-making techniques, Dynasty's strategy was to produce first, negotiate later."[59]

The groundbreaking venture marked the beginning of a new era in Chinese wine production. The landmark deal was followed by several other high-profile ventures with French companies. The Great Wall Wine Company was formed in 1983. This set a precedent that other French winemakers were eager to follow. Pernod Ricard was looking to get in on the act and finally found what they thought would be the right combination in 1988. That was the "Year of the Dragon" according to the Chinese calendar, and it served as inspiration for the name Dragon Seal, a partnership between the Beijing Friendship Winery and Pernod Ricard. They released their first bottle in 1988.[60]

These joint ventures would play a huge role in the ascent of Chinese wine production as Dynasty, Great Wall, and Changyu (the winery founded in 1892, which started the modern wine industry in China) control about sixty percent of all wine sales in China. It is also worth noting that only six companies control about ninety percent of all wine sold in China. These joint ventures were obviously beneficial for the long-term health of the production and sales of wine in China. However, they did not bode nearly as well for their French partners. China has had a long-standing policy underlying industrial expansion

---

[59] Mustacich, *Thirsty Dragon*, 59.

[60] Ibid, 62.

that China retains control of joint ventures with foreign entities. They generally do not want to be giving foreign companies controlling stakes in ventures, perhaps because of how they had been exploited in the colonial era. As a result, the French companies have had difficult and occasionally disastrous experiences in China. The French are often tight-lipped about their miscues. But wine writer George Taber offers this valuable insight from a French insider who agreed to comment with the assurance that he would remain anonymous. The Chinese tend to sign short contracts with French companies in order to glean as much as possible about the proper production of wine. Like the Chinese have in other industries, they reap as much information as possible and then cast aside their partners, implementing the knowledge into their own endeavors. Curiously, this has not deterred other French companies from continuing to enter into contracts with Chinese companies. The most important of these was an agreement between China's biggest state-held investment company CITIC and Domaines Barons de Rothschilds. What makes this deal unique is that the Chinese will have only a thirty percent stake in the venture, bucking the trend of Chinese companies as majority owners. Moreover, the name Rothschild is synonymous the world over for two things: great wine and deep pockets. For this reason, it has the best chance to make history as a triumph for both parties, not just the Chinese.[61]

---

[61] Taber, A Toast to Bargain Wines, 147-148.

This exposes another difficulty that French wine companies have had in China, a difficulty which plagues Chinese wine-makers as well: land ownership. As Barnard Magrez, a well-known *négociant* in Bordeaux once said, when he was discussing the fact that the Chinese government owns all of the land, "even the stones are Chinese."[62] This shows that the ground under these negotiations is constantly shifting, at the whim of the Chinese government, who owns all the land in China (made available for cultivation through leasing). This was also a problem for domestic producers because they had to get their grapes from local farmers. Chinese wine makers have difficulties with resources, including labor, that are unimaginable in the West. Chris Ruffle laments some similar issues as he recounts his tumultuous journey founding Treaty Port Vineyards in the heart of the Shandong province in *A Decent Bottle of Wine in China*.

Although there may be a few rows of vines around major vineyards to set the scenery, most of the grapes are actually produced by small farming operations that sign contracts with the wineries. Peasant farm families will tend to the vines and produce grapes at the behest of the vineyards. But this takes a great deal of control out of the vineyards' hands, making each crop more unpredictable than the wineries' counterparts in, say, California. Not only are small wineries as beholden to this maddening arrangement, but large ones like Dragon Seal must go through this process to get the grapes that they need to produce their wine.[63]

---

[62] Mustacich, *Thirsty Dragon*, 70.

[63] Taber, *A Toast to Bargain Wines*, 153.

Why has the Chinese Wine Industry Grown so Significantly in the Last Twenty Years?

The turn toward capitalism created a new class of Chinese, which was a new rendition of a familiar tune, the *nouveau riche.* These new moneyed Chinese are sometimes referred to as *Tuhao,* and they have a taste for conspicuous consumption: expensive paintings, the finest linens, and of course the world's most sought after wines served as a way to flaunt their wealth. Another reason for this trend, that we must keep in mind, is that the West has often found many fineries from the Orient exotic, and the reverse of this helps to explain China's enthusiasm for crushed European grapes.[64]

The combination of Li Peng's proclamation, essentially ordaining wine in the eyes of the ruling party with its newfound fashionable image, and the demands of the new nouveau riche ignited a fire in the Chinese market that continues to burn brightly today. Since Li's pronouncement, the acceleration of wine appreciation in China and the wine industry has been rapid. Consider this statement made at the end of the twentieth century by Pieter Eijkhoff who intensely studied the Chinese Wine industry in the 1990s for his posthumously published dissertation manuscript, *Wine in China*: "Western-style wines are a new product in China and, at this time, still considered a luxury. Wine connoisseurs remain scarce, and a public that yearns for

---

[64] Noel Shu, *China Through a Glass of Wine* (Cafe con Leche Books, 2016), 12-13.

Western products could provide fertile ground for wine promoters determined to educate future customers."[65]

In the late 1990s, there was a particular group that was consuming the majority of wine in China. As Eijkhoff noted in that period: "The average wine consumer in China is between twenty and thirty-five years old, relatively affluent, and lives in an urban area."[66] This is important to note because even though the most conspicuous consumers of wine at the time were government officials, often drinking pricey bottles of Bordeaux, a larger demographic was taking shape which would push the development of Chinese wine culture. It must be noted that the Chinese middle class was expanding at this time, setting the stage for exponential growth in the twenty-first century. As wealth came into the hands of not only the wealthy but a growing middle class of Chinese, the popularity of wine continued to ascend. This powerful force drove wine consumption.[67]

In a 2011 speech to Asia House in London, award-winning author of *The Chinese Dream: The Rise of the World's Largest Middle Class and What It Means to You*, Helen H. Wang, contended, "The rise of China's middle class is the biggest story of our time." She states that this phenomenon will impact markets all over the world. One of the great lessons she learned in the extensive research that she did for her book

---

[65] Eijkhoff, *Wine in China*, 135.

[66] Ibid., 135.

[67] See Figure 1 in Appendix

was that "Chinese are status-conscious people. They would pay premium prices for products and services that can enhance their 'status'. But for products and services that their neighbors and friends cannot see, they would be very price conscious."[68]

So, they are careful with their money when it comes to comfort and prefer to splurge on items that convey status. This is a key insight into why big ticket French wine has become so fashionable in China. This is part of a larger trend which will make China the largest consumer market by 2020, which is the central reason why she says: "The rise of China's middle class is the biggest story of our time." [69]

She believes that this giant middle class is part of a "Chinese Dream" that has many similarities to the upward mobility associated with the "American Dream." One of the main differences, which is vital to the rise of the Chinese wine industry, is the ascent of hundreds of millions of Chinese consumers into the marketplace who want to buy luxury items, including fine wine. Wang reminds us that Chinese millennials (defined as individuals who were born after 1980 and coming into young adulthood in the early 21st Century) are a large sector of the market with a great deal more money to spend than other groups, such as their American counterparts who are drowning in student debt. By

---

[68] Helen H. Wang, "The Biggest Story of Our Time: The Rise of China's Middle Class," *Forbes*, December 21, 2011,
https://www.forbes.com/sites/helenwang/2011/12/21/the-biggest-story-of-our-time-the-rise-of-chinas-middle-class/.

[69] Ibid.

2020, it is projected that there will be 300 million Chinese millennials, compared to 80 million with money to spend.[70]

Wine is one of their favorite things to spend money on.

Learning from the Wine Venture of a Foreign Businessman in China

In light of the changing tastes, the milieu was set to attract foreign investment. A self-starter like Chris Ruffle who seemed always to have had a profound interest in Asia could feel confident enough to invest. Having never been to Asia, he elected to study Chinese language and philosophy at Oxford, graduating in 1981. He spent a few years casting-about before he started working for a metal trading firm called Wogen Resources in Beijing in 1983 and never looked back. From that time, he spent the majority of his time in Asia (primarily in China). After finding success in finance and adding an ability to speak Japanese to his linguistic arsenal, he changed gears and went to Scotland. He undertook the task of rebuilding a castle in Scotland in 1992 from its dilapidated ruins. He purchased this Scottish castle, which he speculated to have been constructed as early as the 14th century, for £50,024. The undertaking was intense and costly, but he managed to fully restore it in 1996. He lived in the

---

[70] Helen H. Wang, "Two Reasons Chinese Millennials Have More Cash To Burn," *Forbes*, October 9, 2016,
https://www.forbes.com/sites/helenwang/2016/10/09/two-reasons-why-chinese-millennials-have-more-cash-to-burn/.

castle for five years and in the process, he fell in love with the construction of Scottish castles.[71]

This experience gave Ruffle the courage to undertake an even greater feat, starting a winery in Shandong China with a newly constructed Scottish-style castle as the château in 2004. Admittedly, Ruffle had no idea what he was in for. What unfolded over the next decade was an intense trial in which it seemed that nearly everything possible went awry. So what does a polymath like Ruffle do when his mission to create a new winery and Scottish castle in the Chinese countryside go awry? He writes a book about his experiences which reads like a cautionary tale to anyone, especially those with any inkling of an idea that they might want to do business in China. But his account is not without humor and the reader can see that even the most maddening aspects of his escapade leave him undeterred.

He recounts wrangling over the final details of his contract with the government for the land on which the vineyard would be situated along with finalizing the plans for his castle. He reflected that the experience taught him that "contracts are viewed differently in China; they are merely an expression of what both parties think or hope at a particular moment," as he had learned from his experience doing business in this foreign land that these contracts "can be reinterpreted or ignored when circumstances change or prove inconvenient."[72]

---

[71] Chris Ruffle, *A Decent Bottle of Wine in China* (Hong Kong: Earnshaw Books Limited, 2015), 11-23.

[72] Ibid, 25

The signing of the contract turned into a rollicking affair and "as the deal was signed, eating and drinking reached a crescendo...toasts were made with baijiu, which tasted like paint thinner, a local grape wine, and a bottle of whisky...This was all topped off with a tonic wine with a snake curled inside." He concludes this account with good natured sarcasm which must have helped him endure the trials and annoyances that allowed him to finally, as the title suggests, craft A Decent Bottle of Wine in China. He states: "No one can say that I haven't suffered for my art."[73]

Conducting business in China forced Ruffle to engage in seemingly interminable maneuvering with politicians. He observed that the "requirement for the constant maintenance of political *guanxi* (relationships) is taxing and something I never understood before I started this project. My admiration for successful businessmen in China increased."[74]

Any foreigner with dreams of producing wine in China will be well served to read Ruffle's colorful account of founding his own winery in the Shandong province. Aside from his account of producing wine as an individual, there are many important factors for us to look at when it comes to production as a whole.

In addition to Ruffle and other foreigners who have come to China in order to work on wine production and related fields, it must be stressed that many native Chinese are finding success. In China, the

---

[73] Ibid.

[74] Ibid, 39

development of the industry has created tremendous opportunities. One such story is that of Zhang Jing, co-owner of the Helan Qingxue Winery in the Ningxia region, who was named the Winemaker of the Year at the 2013 Chinese RVF wine awards (these annual awards come from the Chinese edition of La Revue du Vin de France magazine). She got there through hard work and innovation. Many now acknowledge her outstanding abilities; her climb to become one of the nation's most celebrated winemakers before the age of forty was not easy and her sagacious advice is simple but reflects what she has learned along the way: "If you want to go into the wine industry, you must make a long-term plan, not be anxious for success." This being said, she asserts that the Chinese industry is still in its infancy with a great deal of room for growth.[75]

---

[75] Shu, *China Through a Glass of Wine*, 117.

CHAPTER VI

Counterfeit Wines and Appellation

Once China began to have larger industrial wine companies, the question of imports and exports became more important. However, before discussing the aspect of doing business in China, understanding the concept of appellation and rampant counterfeiting is in order. Although the concepts might not seem directly related on the surface, they do have some interesting connections that reveal some underlying problems in the Chinese wine industry.

Koch Experiences Counterfeiting Up Close and Personal

Bill Koch is one of the brothers of the Super PAC-creating Arch-Conservative Koch Brothers. In 1983, Bill and his brother Frederick were awarded nearly a billion dollars from their more infamous brothers Charles and David (Bill's fraternal twin brother) as there was an epic family feud over the family business, Koch Industries. The bitter resentment never seemed to subside as Bill filed another subsequent lawsuit against Charles for undervaluing the company in legal battles that spanned more than a decade. Bill would go on to found a $4 billion energy company of his own, the Oxbow Group.[76]

The brothers seemed always to be trying to outdo each other by making statements with their conspicuous consumption. Each had their own predilections. "My brother Charles likes to collect money. My brother David used to like to collect girls until he got married," said Bill in an interview with 60 Minutes.[77]

Bill Koch collects many things including masterpieces by artists like Degas and Monet, but perhaps he is most passionate about wine, evidenced by his world-class wine cellar stocked with about 15,000 bottles, worth tens of millions of dollars.[78]

Perhaps his most famous wine acquisitions were four bottles which allegedly belonged to Thomas Jefferson. Koch purchased these bottles for $100,000 apiece. These bottles were "discovered" by Hardy Rodenstock, a debonair wine collector, who had graced the cover of *Wine Spectator*. The bottles turned out to be fakes, leaving a frustrated

---

[76] Daniel Fisher, "Inside The Koch Empire: How The Brothers Plan To Reshape America," *Forbes*, December 5, 2012, https://www.forbes.com/sites/danielfisher/2012/12/05/inside-the-koch-empire-how-the-brothers-plan-to-reshape-america/.

[77] Sharyn Alfonsi, "Billionaire Koch Brother's Crusade against Counterfeit Wine," CBS News, October 22, 2017, https://www.cbsnews.com/news/billionaire-koch-brothers-crusade-against-counterfeit-wine/.

[78] Ibid.

Koch with little recourse but legal action. In the end, Koch won a judgement against Rodenstock in excess of $1 million.[79]

The revelation that he had been sold fake bottles allegedly belonging to Jefferson encouraged Koch to reassess his wine cellar, and he turned up over four hundred ersatz bottles of wine. Nearly half of those could be traced to one man, Rudy Kurniawan, a smooth operator from Indonesia who was ethnically Chinese. Kurniawan quickly made a name for himself in the elite wine circles of Los Angeles as a generous wine connoisseur with a sophisticated palate. He became a staple at wine auctions throughout the U.S.

Often men in Koch's uncomfortable position try to find discreet ways to handle these situations. Koch explains why so few wine grifters are nabbed: "There is a code of silence in this business because obviously, the faker doesn't want anybody to know that he's making fake wine. The auction house doesn't wanna know that, and then, the collector himself generally doesn't wanna know it. Or if he finds out, he wants to find a secret way to dump it and get his money back. And that's why, you see, I was very unique in being the one who said, 'I'm gonna stand up for it. I'm gonna shine a bright light on these fakers.'"[80]

His pride would compel him to spend over $35 million tracking down those who had duped him. Perhaps years of being taken advantage of by his brothers had forged Koch into a man who refused

---

[79] Ibid.

[80] Ibid.

to be intimidated or deceived. Koch himself reflected on why he was so vigilant in tracking down those who had sold him fakes: "Probably 'cause I had bigger brothers who were always beating up on me, faking me, cheating me a little bit. Maybe that's a part of it."[81]

Before he crossed paths with Bill Koch, Kurniawan had earned a reputation as a playboy who sold millions of dollars of wine at auction while living in a multi-million dollar mansion in Arcadia, California (a suburb of Los Angeles). On March 8, 2012, FBI agents stormed the mansion to find a wine-counterfeiting workshop in full production with empty wine bottles, carefully tattered wine labels and all the other supplies used to hoodwink collectors like Koch. Kurniawan was found guilty of a battery of charges including counterfeiting, bank fraud, and falsely claiming to be a legal US resident without immigration status, and he is currently serving a ten year sentence in federal prison.[82]

His story is recounted in the highly entertaining Netflix documentary, "Sour Grapes." In the film, it is speculated that thousands of fake bottles can be traced to Kurniawan, which caused some experts to speculate that he had help producing the spurious bottles in his homeland of Indonesia. Kurniawan's arrest was the largest penalty ever handed down in the US for fake wines, and it was the first ever such case pursued by the United States Department of Justice. The moment marked a revelation of how high stakes wine

---

[81] Ibid.

[82] "Rare Wine Dealer Sentenced in Counterfeiting Scheme," Story, Federal Bureau of Investigation, September 5, 2014, https://www.fbi.gov/news/stories/rare-wine-dealer-sentenced-in-counterfeiting-scheme.

auctions had become, and unmasked the shadowy underworld that parallels the big-dollar collectors pursuing the finest wines on the planet. The public was able to peer into the place where big dollars are spent without certainty of authenticity with some similarities to the world of fine art. The fortunes spent on these hallmarks of high culture create incentives for forgery and call to mind the truism that if enough money is involved, graft is sure to follow. This was a huge revelation in the United States about a thriving illicit industry. This industry had been growing in China for more than a decade before the Kurniawan story came to light.

In China, Fake Wine Has Become a Thriving Industry

No discussion about wine in China is complete without a look into the massive counterfeit wine industry. This industry not only affects wine producers but also consumers. The picture of Chinese wine is not complete without delving into this issue.

China has long been known as the land of counterfeit goods, from DVDs to Rolex watches. There are Chinese knockoffs in markets from New York to Beijing. Alas, Chinese counterfeiters were not only faking luxury goods, but even unconscionable items such as baby formula. Such practices have been alarmingly common during China's industrial expansion. Wine is no exception. In fact, bogus wine production has become a booming industry in China. After the turn of the second millennium, when the red wine craze was gaining momentum in China, the land of knock-offs added a new wrinkle: counterfeits. There developed a great demand in the world market for ersatz fine wine, much of it Chinese "Bordeauxs," a phenomenon that is well documented in Suzanne Mustacich's eloquent account of the Chinese infatuation with France's most fabled region in *Thirsty Dragon* which bears the telling subtitle: China's Lust for Bordeaux and the Threat to the World's Best Wines. By 2013, it was estimated that half of the wine in China could be fake. This opened up a bizarre parallel market where "professional bottle recyclers" would pay up to $300 for particular bottles such as the Chateau Lafite-Rothschild without any wine in them![83]

This led to the now routine practice that bottles are shattered after consumption to ensure that the bottles would not be refilled with potentially harmful dreck that could lead to serious illness. However, this also opened a new market for savvy cheats who fabricated replica bottles and pressed on their own fake labels. The counterfeiters always seemed to find ways to practice their ingenuity and stay ahead.[84]

The name Rothschild is recognized the world over, and the family's wine production has produced some of the most expensive and arguably the best wines in the world. The name Lafite offers a curious insight into the Chinese wine industry and the mindset of the Chinese consumer. Barons de Rothschild Lafite wines have long been prized

---

[83] MacNeil, *The Wine Bible*, 915.

[84] Ibid.

with certain vintages fetching thousands of dollars. The name Lafite translates roughly as "hillock" in English. But the name Lafite is also attached to a number of Bordeaux's celebrated First Growths.[85] The name Lafite has long been intertwined with the history of wine. In fact, the most expensive wine purchased was a 1787 Lafite, once owned by Thomas Jefferson, by billionaire Malcolm Forbes in 1985. It was widely believed that this bottle was a fake and the transaction led to years of litigation, a situation that was the theme of Benjamin Wallace's *The Billionaire's Vinegar: The Mystery of the World's Most Expensive Bottle of Wine*. The tale of this bottle of Lafite is interestingly related to Bill Koch's pursuit of counterfeiters due to his purchase of four bottles that also allegedly belonged to Jefferson. Nevertheless, the entire web of connections is beyond the scope of this book, but it is well worth the inquiry for both education and entertainment value.[86]

For our purposes, the important part is that the packaging and often the backstory play a huge role in how the wine is valued. So, of course people are going to try to cash in when people are spending hundreds of thousands of dollars. This cheeky comment by British oenophile Michael Broadbent captures some of the psychology of packaging, prejudice, and the expectations of a taster: "A sight of the label is worth fifty years' experience. A cynical truism, for what an impressionable lot we are! Even the most disciplined taster is biased by the mere glimpse of

---

[85] This is the highest ranking for a chateau according to the 1855 Classification, which will be described at length later.

[86] Taber, *A Toast to Bargain Wines*, 7.

a label, even the shape of the bottle."[87] Imagine the pull of the label on an absolute novice with money to spend and people to impress. Jancis Robinson echoes this sentiment: "It is absolutely staggering how important a part the label plays in the business of tasting. If we know that a favorite region, producer or vintage is coming up, we automatically start relishing it—giving it every benefit of tasting doubt."[88] This was also the subject for the critically acclaimed book *The Wine Trials* written by Robin Goldstein.

Chinese consumers of wine have been known to be taken in by the power of the label just like the rest of us. However, the obsession with the name Lafite took this tendency to hysterical levels, even though what "lafite" is really referring to is simply the hills that a given vineyard or Chateau may be attached to. To the Chinese consumer, the name Lafite is easily recognizable and is associated with quality, although the name may have nothing to do with the actual quality of the wine in that bottle. The result is that many bottles of wine boast the Lafite name on the label, but that does not reflect the quality nor necessarily the origin of the wine inside, and these efforts knowingly mislead people in the marketplace.

Nick Bartman's Big Find

Nick Bartman, Director at Intellectual Property Protection Co., has worked undercover, artfully passing himself off as other nationalities

---

[87] Quoted in Taber, *A Toast to Bargain Wines*, 6.

[88] Quoted in Taber, *A Toast to Bargain Wines*, 6.

playing roles like the corrupt businessman for twenty-six years. He has made a career spotting forgeries, and his unique work has had him traipsing across Asia, chasing networks of counterfeiters. But nothing was quite like what he found in China's illicit wine industry. As he reflected on his experiences in the criminal underworld of counterfeit goods, he stated: "Throughout all these experiences, and raiding many hundreds of companies with the police, my body compass was forever pointing to China, the de facto center of counterfeits."[89]

Bartman was working for the Bordeaux Wine Council (CIVB) when he was digging deeper into the shadowy world of the trade in faux-French wine. At this time, a wave of police raids of counterfeiters were becoming better known to the population. In December of 2010, when the buzz about phony bottles of French wine in China was elevating and the topic of counterfeit wine was heating up as a news item, China Central Television (CCTV) released a documentary about the illicit wine trade in December of 2010. A manager, interviewed in the piece, confessed that certain wines in Qingdao were comprised of 20% juice from fermented grapes, while the balance was water, sugar, and a combination of dangerous chemicals. Some of the chemicals in the bogus wine were known to cause irregular heartbeats, headaches, and in the most extreme cases, cancer. This revelation ignited a shockwave that coursed through law enforcement and resulted in a new round of raids.[90]

---

[89] Quoted in Mustacich, *Thirsty Dragon*, 130.

[90] Mustacich, *Thirsty Dragon*, 138.

The report led to the eventual arrests of six people, including life imprisonment for the most serious offender, and the closing of three offending wineries. The report, punishments made, and the arrests were part of a serious crackdown on counterfeit products in 2010 through an operation called Bright Sword. This made Bartman's job, to seek justice for the CIVB, easier. The stakes were high; Bartman reckoned that the total value of the ersatz wine operations he was targeting was in the neighborhood of $37 million. The CIVB sought to pull the French embassy in Beijing into the operation. They were joined by members of the Chinese General Administration of Quality Supervision, Inspection, and Quarantine, while Bartman presented his case. After seeing the massive amount of evidence Bartman had compiled, the Chinese officials elected to aid in the investigation with a full task force that would give them the teeth to exact some justice. They busted a large ring of counterfeiters, finally able to execute after Bartman had worked so doggedly to gather evidence and build an ironclad case. After their huge confiscation, a sampling of questionable bottles was sent to France to determine the nature of the contents. However, the bottles were mysteriously destroyed, and when the Chinese sent more wine to the French for testing, the results were written in cryptic French lingo that baffled Chinese authorities. Although Bartman was convinced the wine was fake and a high level fraud was taking place, he was frustratingly impotent in the process. He was sickened by what happened. "What started out to be the perfect storm resulted in nothing more than mediocrity, with lost opportunities in France as well as China. Our long-term damage to counterfeiters was estimated at €30 million, but this was low compared with what could have been achieved," he reflected. "Worse still, the Chinese government's legal actions against counterfeiters were hampered by the shenanigans in France."[91]

Nick Bartman's investigation is an instructive case that reflects many of the nuances of the counterfeiting wine culture in China. Wine is big business, and where there is a lot of money to be made, the counterfeiters will flock. But his investigation was swept up into the crazy whirlwind surrounding counterfeiting in China, where the bad guys seemed always to be at least one step ahead of the law. He knew that many smaller vineyards in Bordeaux were seeing profits bled away by unscrupulous con men. Unless they all united against these swindlers, there would be little hope of eradicating the trade in faux Bordeaux all together. In his expert opinion, "Counterfeit control is a mental game with the bad guys." The score is not completely settled, but there are renewed efforts that involve smashing bottles of frequently counterfeited wines after tastings and using high-tech labeling to make labels on bottles that are much more difficult to reproduce. We shall see if the tide will turn against those who profit from deception and the "mental game" can be won.[92]

---

[91] Ibid, 139-153.

[92] Ibid, 156.

The Fake Wine Continues to Flow

So far, those who have sought to stop wine counterfeiting in China have been ultimately unsuccessful. At least the CIVB shone a light on a dangerous operation taking place in the dark corners of China's counterfeiting culture, exposing criminals who were passing off dangerous concoctions of wine. Further, Nick Bartman exposed high-level fraud, even though their efforts did little to stem the flow of fake wine in China. The shadowy industry continues to grow at an astonishing pace.

In 2017, the China Policy Institute assessed the counterfeit wine situation and estimated that 70% of the wine in China is fake. This startling figure exposes a situation that is currently out of control, and they see no end in sight when it comes to stopping the rampant forgeries. The study found that even though the government is fighting back, it is just too out of control to stop. The report concluded, rather ominously, that "As long as a market for fake wine exists, it seems inevitable that the problem will persist."[93]

Appellation in China

Then there is the sticky situation of appellation. Appellation has had a major impact on the industry worldwide. The question of Appellation

---

[93] Anqi Shen, "Fake Wine in China," *Asia Dialogue* (blog), January 16, 2017, http://theasiadialogue.com/2017/01/16/fake-wine-in-china/.

in China was inevitable, and how it is resolved has major ramifications for the industry, including the counterfeit wine industry.

Given the pervasive reputation for counterfeiting, there is a stigma that attaches itself to many Chinese products in the West, not just wine. In fact, the Chinese themselves are wary of their wine. In a recent study, Chinese consumers were asked to compare Chinese wine to foreign wine. They responded by saying that in comparison, many Chinese wines were "polluted" and "adulterated." On the other hand, the foreign wine was perceived as superior because "they control the production process strictly and use fewer chemical additives." As the Chinese buyers become more educated, they learn to scrutinize the labels for clues of quality and control.[94]

David Henderson was an engineer from the U.S. who had found some success running a store called Montrose Food & Wine in Beijing. But after helping Jess Jackson (of Kendall-Jackson) search for a place to make wine in China, he was instantly taken with the Ningxia Hui Autonomous Region when the two of them landed and visited there for a reconnaissance mission. As he said of this magical moment, "When the jet landed in Ningxia, our search for the ideal location to grow grapes in China was over." The honeymoon was short as Henderson ran into a number of frustrations while trying to get his wine venture off the ground. When he acquired a deeper understanding of the industry, he was close to despair. He realized what was missing: regulation. He knew that if there were no standards for quality, then

---

[94] Akalin and Lazar, *Wine in China*, location 231.

there could not be an ability to export or be taken seriously on the international scene. So, he set out to get the area around his winery, Dragon's Hollow in the Helan Mountains, designated like an appellation. The officials in the Ningxia region were clueless about what he wanted. He then consulted with the state-owned enterprise he had dealt with when he owned his food and wine store in Beijing, hoping that they could help him further his cause. He contacted the Washington D.C. rep of the Chinese Ministry of Agriculture and discussed getting a designation like an appellation for his part of Ningxia, and he also tapped numerous contacts he had within the Chinese government from his time in Beijing. [95]

In 2008, after five years of inquiries from Washington D.C. to Beijing, Henderson got word that there would be a standard for wines coming from the authorized area in the Helan Mountains where Dragon's Hollow made its home. "We were the ones directly responsible for creating the Eastern Foot of the Helan Mountain appellation," reflected Henderson. "I believe it was the first appellation in China, and we were only able to get this done [through] a combination of Beijing and Washington." It is important to reiterate that Henderson's Dragon's Hollow is one of the few Chinese wines to find some success in the U.S. market.[96]

Given the pervasiveness of counterfeit wine in China, appellation has special significance in the industry. However, it is but one mark of

---

[95] Mustacich, *Thirsty Dragon*, 71-72.

[96] Ibid.

authenticity as people in the industry continue to search for a way to authenticate and ensure that the premium wine China produces is not besmirched by the never-ending flow of counterfeit wine. This could be a key part of the industry as China seeks to export more of the wine it produces.

CHAPTER VII

Global Considerations Regarding Chinese Wines

Importing

Wine became so popular in China by the late 1990s that demand far outpaced domestic production. The importation of foreign wine increased nearly tenfold between 1995 and 1998.[97] This increase paralleled the continuation of rapid economic growth, creating a new class of Chinese with money to spend and a taste for Western luxury goods. As Patricio de la Fuente Saez, a director of a Hong Kong wine distributor called Link, said, "People want a fridge, a car, and a bottle of wine on the table. It means you've arrived."[98]

This also speaks to a very important aspect that anyone who wants to understand the wine industry in China must grasp. The profile of the wine consumer has undergone a major change in the last twenty years and the demographics of the average Chinese wine consumer

---

[97] See Figure 3 in Appendix.

[98] Baker, "The Sweet Taste of Success," 1.

continues to change at a rapid pace. In the mid-1990s, the vanguard of wine consumers and wine importers were Chinese of means, willing to pay top dollar for expensive wine with names they recognized. The Chinese consumers' emphasis on name was one reason why such a flourishing counterfeit wine industry grew in China. The desire for well-known names in wine, as Mustacich masterfully recounts in *Thirsty Dragon*, was led by expensive imports from Bordeaux. However, as it started to catch on, the consumption of wine became much more pervasive and egalitarian. As Chinese consumers became more sophisticated about wine, it was no longer a gift to give to diplomats for *gei mianzi*, nor was it about conspicuous consumption. Chinese consumers began to buy wine because they enjoyed it, and they became savvy enough to know how to get the best bang for their yuan.[99]

In fact, Vinexpo, which is the premier event for people in the spirits and wine industry, was launched in Bordeaux in 1981 and is held in uneven years. In 1998 they launched Vinexpo Asia-Pacific, and they held the expo in Hong Kong in 2016. Vinexpo also commissions studies regarding important trends in the industry. Vinexpo is a leader in predicting wine trends and has a finger on the pulse of the industry. They made some bold predictions for the future of wine consumption based upon the current trends in China. China will account for 72% of the growth in the wine imports in the world by 2020. They are projected to overtake the United Kingdom to become the second most valuable wine market by 2020 with a 40% growth between 2016 and

---

[99] Mustacich, *Thirsty Dragon*, 262-269.

2020 compared to a 0.2% growth in the UK during the same period. This puts into perspective how large the predicted growth is for the Chinese market in the next few years. It is a large nation with an increasing thirst for fermented grapes. It is important for us to put in perspective how big the Chinese market is.[100]

About 20 percent of the world's population resides in China which makes it only mildly surprising that the nation became the fifth nation in the world with regards to wine consumption according to the International Organisation of Vine and Wine (OIV). What is shocking is how rapidly wine is becoming the favorite alcoholic drink of choice to sate the thirst of The Red Dragon nation. This becomes even more important when one considers that consumption doubled between 2008 and 2013. This is the kind of increase, combined with the major projected growth by 2020, that cannot be ignored when assessing the future of international wine trade.[101]

The Chinese wine industry has been scaling-up their production to meet demand. According to the OIV, production almost doubled between 1995 and 2012.[102] It is important to note that not all wine produced in China is derived from homegrown grapes, as many are still imported.[103] Even though China continues to import increasing

---

[100] *Vinexpo Newsroom*, "*China Is a Leading Wine Market of the Future.*"

[101] MacNeil, *The Wine Bible*, 908-909.

[102] See Figure 2 in Appendix.

[103] MacNeil, 909-910.

volumes of wine from the rest of the world, more than 80% of the wine consumed in China is produced at home.[104]

Exporting

Tiny amounts of Chinese wine are exported. Dynasty Fine Wines, one of China's largest producers, exports around one percent of their wine.[105] However, some of the wineries have been trying to bust into other markets. Dragon's Hollow, a winery in the Helan Mountains, has found limited distribution in California. Also, Dragon Seal has tried to reproduce the success of the straw-clad bottles of Chianti that were the rage in checkered-tablecloth Italian restaurants in the United States in the 1970s. They have tried placing their product in Chinese restaurants, but it has not seen anything remotely approaching the success of Chianti in the U.S. Perhaps one reason for this is the fact that the Chinese have not been pairing wine with food for a very long time and even for U.S. residents, this concept could take some time getting used to. Most Chinese restaurants usually offer their fare with Tsing Tao beer or rice wine.[106]

---

[104] Jason Chow, "China Is Now World's Biggest Consumer of Red Wine," *WSJ* (blog), January 29, 2014, https://blogs.wsj.com/scene/2014/01/29/china-is-now-worlds-biggest-consumer-of-red-wine/.

[105] Agence France-Presse, "'China Will Rock Our Wine World' But Needs Time," *Wine-Searcher*, June 2, 2014, https://www.wine-searcher.com/m/2014/06/china-will-rock-our-wine-world.

[106] Taber, *A Toast to Bargain Wines*, 142.

Shipping Wine to and From China

Bottled wine is a heavy product that can be costly to ship. The logistics are such that for most of the time, air delivery is simply too expensive. In the past, sea was the undisputed way to ship wine to China because of the relatively lower cost and the fact that with China's great rivers and waterways, it is relatively easy to transfer the cargo within China. Even so, a comparatively miniscule amount of wine is shipped out of China. Although most ports have adequate storage facilities, most are not climate controlled, which can be perilous for wine. Stories abound of shipments of thousands of bottles either sitting in the sun or a hot warehouse for months, spoiling the wine for consumption.[107]

In 2012, the first Trans-Eurasian rail began regular service. Since then, China has invested heavily in creating a sophisticated system of more than forty lines connecting fifteen cities in Europe with over forty in China. As a result, the volume of cargo has doubled annually. This is essentially the modern version of the Silk Road, updated with tools to skyrocket its capacity and efficiency.[108]

The first cases of wine left Duisburg, Germany in May of 2017, and arrived in Yiwu, China just under a month later. The wine was shipped in cars lined with a special foil insulation, regulating both the humidity

---

[107] Eijkhoff, *Wine in China*, 147.

[108] Wade Shepard, "How European Wine Is Now Going To China Aboard Silk Road Trains," *Forbes*, July 23, 2017, https://www.forbes.com/sites/wadeshepard/2017/07/23/europe-on-the-new-silk-road-european-wine-can-now-be-shipped-to-china-by-rail/.

and temperature inside. The wine arrived unspoiled. This ensures that the volume of wine carried between Europe and China by train will certainly increase as Eurasian rail trade continues to mature. But it will not replace other methods of transport. JF Hillebrand is a freight forwarder of alcoholic beverages, which is a company that arranges the logistics for producers looking to get their goods to final destinations. They were involved in the initial shipment of wine to China from Europe. JF Hillebrand's director for China, Jannson Chan, stated, "This solution complements sea freight and air freight; it is by no means a replacement to these solutions." He then added, "However, given the current difficult context for shipping lines—instability, unavailability, increasing prices—it means more options not only for big European wine makers but also for Chinese importers."[109]

Foreign Businessmen in China

Doing business in China can be challenging, especially as a foreigner. Businessmen who are planning to distribute wine in China and working with other aspects of Chinese business in this giant multicultural country for the first time will quickly find that it is far different than dealings in the West. First, there are the obvious obstacles when conducting business in a challenging language and navigating foreign cultural mores. Fortunately, Mandarin has become ubiquitous in China and beyond, and it is not hard to find help with

---

[109] Ibid.

translation at a reasonable price. The mechanics of doing so are beyond the scope of this book. However, a quick lesson in etiquette can save hours of frustration and increase the success of a given venture. What follows is meant to be a sip that will whet the palate and set the ground for further inquiry.

As mentioned before, *guanxi (relationships) and gei mianzi* (face and status) are important in several facets of Chinese life, especially in business. Without getting too deep into defining these terms, which have been defined before, it is important for us to see how they work together in the business world of China.

Establishing a business relationship is key to having success with Chinese business ventures, and it is a bit more arduous and certainly different than what most Western business people are used to. Chris Ruffle, for example, went into detail about the many various hoops he had to jump through, including lavish dinners which included such acts of faith as eating donkey and drinking a concoction with a snake curled inside. He also alluded to the fact that, on several occasions, he had to spend a great deal of money to entertain officials and business associates. The sentiment that it might be difficult and expensive to gain some momentum in a Chinese business venture is echoed by sommelier Noel Shu, who says that "A typical business dinner can run as high as $500 and a typical night out, as much as $750."[110]

So, one should expect an upfront cost and maneuvering as par for the course in China. No savvy businessman does a deal in a foreign

---

[110] Shu, *China Through a Glass of Wine*, 74.

country without the guarantee of a contract. Of course, a contract is the bedrock of any business deal. However, even the nature of contracts is different in China. Ruffle found the contracts were not honored in the same way he was accustomed to in the West, as the other party made changes that would seem dishonest to people doing business in say the US or UK. This is not unusual says Noel Shu, who states: "Unlike in the West, contracts are considered fluid in China and are subject to change later based on circumstances." His advice is to stay "playful" and to be "open-minded" because he asserts that their "intention is not to be deceptive, but to realize the best deal."[111]

If this sounds stressful, perhaps doing business in China is not for you. But if you do decide to take the leap and distribute wine in China or undertake some other venture, Shu warns, "China is simply not structured to allow unfettered international presence without boots on the ground."[112]

Jeff Harder, co-owner of Ex Nihilo Vineyards, had an interesting time trying to break into the Chinese market. He was one of the rare Canadian wineries to seek distribution in the Far East. What he found was that the process was arduous, but the potential rewards were worth fighting for. Not only did he secure distribution in Japan, but also in China. But it is not something that came overnight, due to the slower process of building trust and the unique dance that business people

---

[111] Ibid, 75-76.

[112] Ibid, 73.

must undertake to get distributions. He warns those who are looking for the quick kill to stay away or adjust their expectations, "Don't think you're going to run over there tomorrow and find somebody to distribute your wines." [113]

In the long run he found that doing business in Hong Kong is a little different, perhaps because of the Western influence there. He reflected, "It's faster than mainland China, but they're still cautious before making any large commitments." If one is trying to break into distribution in China, it is important to do two major things. First, do as much homework as possible with regards to the language, culture, logistics, etc. before considering boarding a plane. Second, change your mindset and lower your expectations to the speed at which the business will develop and how the transaction will unfold. But in the end, it is such a large and blossoming market that it cannot be ignored. As Harder reflects, with the tone of a wily veteran, "With patience comes success."[114]

However, patience does not necessarily guarantee success. "Due to the vastness of China and the grand scale of its wine market, few North American wineries can hope to have a significant presence across the country. For most of them, what they need to do is find the right niche."[115]

---

[113] Kate Lavin, "The Slow Boat to China," *Wines & Vines*, January 2012, http://www.winesandvines.com/features/95708.

[114] Ibid.

[115] Shu, *China Through a Glass of Wine*, 79.

In an article about doing business in China, Kate Lavin, managing editor of *Wines & Vines*, opines, "Unlike French chateaus, which sell bottles for exorbitant prices at upscale restaurants in Shanghai and Hong Kong, U.S. and Canadian wineries can find themselves lumped in with other New World wine producers." So, on the one hand, China's traditional Francophilia when it comes to crushed grapes is a sizable obstacle to overcome which makes it hard for North American wineries to compete at the high end of the Chinese wine market. On the other hand, there is a thirst for bulk wine imported from Australia, South America, and Spain where the production costs tend to be lower, making it hard for many North American and Western European countries to compete at the lower end of the market.[116] As Jeff Harder, co-owner of Ex Nihilo vineyards in British Columbia, points out, "Distributors go into other world markets and buy Argentine and Chilean wines for amazing prices, as we know those countries can offer." This trend means that there is little wiggle room for many wineries in North America and Western Europe when it comes to breaking into the Chinese market.[117]

Why Does China Export so Little Wine?

The first reason that China does not export much wine is that it is hard for them to compete in the world market because their world-class wines are

---

[116] See Figure 4 in Appendix.

[117] Lavin, "The Slow Boat to China."

created by boutique vineyards and the cost of production creates a problem in the value when compared to other wines around the world.

The second reason is that with a population of about 1.4 billion people and a growing taste for wine, much of the local production is consumed at home, so there is no need to spend the money to break into other markets. As Jim Boyce observed, "There's far more money to be made at home than in selling abroad."[118]

As mentioned before, the "Big Three"—Changyu, Great Wall, and Dynasty Wines—lead production in China because they own the majority of the country's wineries, and the International Business Times estimated in 2015 that they had a whopping $8 billion in revenue.[119]

However, although the "Big Three" have plenty of business at home, they are not averse to expanding their reach. Michael Wu, vice-chairman of the Chengdu-based Chinese Wine Associations Alliance (CWAA), stated in an interview with China Daily: "[The Big Three] want to go to the US, but they don't really have the capability now. In other words, they want to go to any market that would accept them." He was quick to add that supplying the burgeoning market in China was enough to satisfy their needs in the foreseeable future.[120]

---

[118] Michelle FlorCruz, "China's Wine Industry Explodes, But Not Yet On The World Stage," *International Business Times*, May 3, 2015, http://www.ibtimes.com/chinas-wine-industry-explodes-not-yet-world-stage-1902284.

[119] Ibid.

[120] Jack Friefelder and Bian Jibu, "Wine in the US: 'Made in China' Is Rare," *China Daily* USA, October 30, 2015, http://usa.chinadaily.com.cn/epaper/2015-10/30/content_22325719.htm.

Why Is There Not a Lot of Wine Exported to the United States and Europe?

The United States has long been aware of the potential of the Chinese wine business and has sought to become a major player in their development. Consider this excerpt from the U.S. Congressional record in 1996:

> While only about one-fifth of China's current grape harvest is made into wine, the potential for wine production and consumption is enormous.
>
> Importing and exporting wine is gaining the attention of the newly emerging economic structures of China and foreign investors and partnerships. Both Chinese government and private-sector wine interests are eager to welcome and learn from American viticulture and enology techniques and methodologies.
>
> Thus, with an invitation from the Government of the People's Republic of China and through the sponsorship of the Citizen Ambassador Program of People to People International, our Viticulture and Enology Delegation of one French and eleven American wine experts, representing all sectors of the wine industry, visited China, April 14 to 27, 1996. This was the first official U.S. wine Delegation to travel to China since 1949. A previous Viticulture and Enology Delegation was cancelled the day before departure in June of 1989 due to the Tiananmen Square incident.
>
> The mission of the Delegation was to meet with counterpart contacts at all levels of the Chinese wine industry; exchange information; discuss topics of mutual interest such as vineyard management, winemaking technology, viticulture-enology research

and training, sales and marketing strategies, government regulatory oversight, foreign investment and joint venture opportunities, import and export potentials, and tariff rate issues; establish ongoing professional and business relationships; and, generally, assess the status of development and growth potential of the wine industry in the People's Republic of China.[121]

The report continued to outline an itinerary that included stops in major cities such as Beijing and Shanghai, including a meeting with the PRC leaders, export and import companies, educational institutions, and vineyards. They stated that the objective of the "Citizen Ambassador Program" was to "make friends and promote greater understanding among professional and concerned individuals internationally, in this case between the wine communities of the United States and the People's Republic of China." Joint ventures were considered a major tactic in the overall strategy. They considered the trip a success, believing that they had made major inroads that would yield a large increase in the export to China of U.S. products in general and wine in particular. They stressed that "patience and long-term commitment are necessary." The report ended on an encouraging note, stating: "Bottom line: If there is money to be made by Chinese involved individuals and/or businesses in marketing and selling an American product (wine), success will eventually happen!"[122]

---

[121] Eijkhoff, *Wine in China*, 151-152.

[122] Eijkhoff, *Wine in China*, 152-153.

China joined the World Trade Organization (WTO) in December 2001, marking a significant step forward for U.S.-Chinese trade, which was already on the rise. In fact, U.S. imports from China nearly doubled from 1996-2001, rising from $51.5 billion to $102 billion in 2001. In the same period, exports rose from $12 billion to $19 billion. The WTO had a major impact on trade as the increase in imports from 2001 to 2016 was $102 billion to $462 billion and exports from $19 billion to $116 billion.[123]

---

[123] US Census Bureau Foreign Trade Division, "Foreign Trade: Data," United States Census Bureau, May 21, 2018, https://www.census.gov/foreign-trade/balance/c5700.html#2001.

CHAPTER VIII

Wine Tourism in China

When planning a trip to China, one envisions parades of people carrying dragon kites in Beijing, monks practicing martial arts atop misty mountains, and rivers dotted with colorful junks in full sail. What does not come to mind is wine enthusiasts standing around a bar in a tasting room, while swirling glasses of merlot, and discussing the finer points of viticulture. As we have seen on our journey so far, this aspect is rapidly changing as China continues to emerge as a destination for wine tourism.

Wine Bars

As wine culture continues to develop, Chinese tipplers continue to look for places to enjoy wine. Wine bars have been popping up all over China to feed the growing demand from people who like to go out and enjoy the night by discovering new wines and revisiting old favorites. Of all the cities in China that are embracing wine culture, the wine bar scene is certainly biggest in Beijing, Shanghai, and Hong Kong.

If you visit these cities, you will certainly have ample opportunity to sample some great wine. Here are some of the most popular wine bars in China that you cannot miss if searching for a great place to savor a glass of red. Following is a brief guide to some of the best wine bars in Hong Kong, Shanghai, and Beijing to whet your palate.

Wine Bars in Hong Kong

Hong Kong has a burgeoning wine scene that has produced many fantastic wine bars. Tastings Wine Bar is routinely rated among the absolute best wine bars in all of Hong Kong. If you visit this lively haunt, you won't have to wonder why. The restrained modern interior is comfortable, and the emphasis of the entire operation is completely on the wine.

Tastings is the perfect destination for wine lovers who enjoy comparing and contrasting a variety of great wines. They feature forty of their 160+ wines at a time on their Enomatic wine dispenser. They pour full glasses (150 milliliters) as well as half glasses, and for those who would simply like a taste, you can purchase 25 ml of wine to get a sense of its character before diving in with a bottle.

Spoon has an excellent reputation for outstanding French cuisine. But this restaurant, located at the Intercontinental Hotel in Hong Kong, has become equally famous for their wine selection. Visitors need not reserve a table to enjoy their selection of over 550 wines from all corners of the globe. There is an open bar where guests can sit and open a bottle of superb wine and see where the night leads.

Wine Bars on the Mainland

If you're in Shanghai and are looking for the perfect place to escape for a glass of wine with your special someone, then look no further than Dr. Wine. The two-floor establishment is a sight to behold with exposed brick, attractive leather furniture, and romantic lighting. The wine list is extensive, and it has something for the bargain hunter as well as the connoisseur looking for the perfect bottle of high-end French red.

Enoterra Shanghai is the original Entorra in China, predating the sister wine bar in Beijing. It is the oldest wine bar in Shanghai and has a solid reputation for their selection and the expertise of their staff. They run a daily happy hour with deals on glasses of wine. Also, they offer a fabulous menu featuring delicious tapas which are a perfect accompaniment to a glass of crushed grapes, including Salmon Tartar and homemade foie gras.

Riding high after the success in Shanghai, Enoterra Beijing has become the wine bar in China's capital city. Established in 2007 by two wine importation companies, Enoterra is committed to bringing the finest wines from around the world to their guests' glasses. The candle-lit, intimate setting makes it an ideal place to unwind with a date after a full day of seeing the sights of Beijing. They run a daily happy hour from 4-8 PM when they offer 50% off wines by the glass, which is the perfect way to whet your appetite before dinner.

With over a hundred carefully selected bottles to choose from, there is something for everyone. Also, the staff at Enoterra is passionate about wine and happy to share their vast knowledge with guests. It is no wonder why *Time Out Beijing* says that in the capital city this popular haunt "is heads and shoulders above the competition."

A Final Word on Wine Bars

The proliferation of good wine bars in China is a sign of the times. As wine continues to grow in popularity in the nation, there are more ways to enjoy the coveted beverage. Most major cities in China now have at least one wine bar, but the three cities mentioned here are definitely the center of the action when it comes to drinking at wine bars, with new ones frequently emerging.

However, there are many other amazing wine experiences to be had if you venture into wine regions such as the Ningxia Hui Autonomous Region and Shandong where you can tipple right at the vineyards. No matter how you like to enjoy wine, China has something new and exciting for every oenophile.

The Wine Regions of China

The following is a brief review of the provinces in China. Each has a contribution to the wine scene and has its own unique allures for the tourist.

Shandong Province

Although the rapid increase of wine consumption in China is a relatively new phenomenon, it is not without historical precedent. In the 1990s, archaeologists unearthed clay pots in the Shandong Province containing residue from wine made from grapes (along with honey and rice). These containers were dated around 2,500 BCE. Yet, drinking fermented grapes has not been a fixture in Chinese culture until recently, as we have seen.[124]

Wine appreciation in Shandong dates back to the sixth century BCE, when it is alleged that Confucius occasionally enjoyed sampling the local wine. The Confucian heritage was no accident because Shandong is a great place for wine production as Chang Bishi discovered in the nineteenth century. The province is essentially what California is to the United States, a beautiful region with an unparalleled climate. The coastal region has nutrient-rich, loose soil which is well-ventilated, making it an agricultural center. The mildness of the climate allows for grapes to be grown without having to deal with the freezing that can destroy vines in the colder Northern wine-producing regions. According to wine guru Gerard Colin, Shandong has the most profound possibilities when it comes to producing the finest wine in China.[125]

The province can be considered the cradle of the modern wine industry in China because this is where Chang Bishi elected to found his Changyu Wine Production Company in Yantai in 1892. This also meant that the subsequent wine makers in the region could benefit from being near the most state-of-the-art winemaking processes and equipment.

---

[124] MacNeil, *The Wine Bible*, 908.

[125] Taber, *A Toast to Bargain Wines*, 150-151.

No region produces more volume than Shandong. The oceanic climate is conducive to cultivating European grape varieties and contributes to making it the center of the modern-day wine movement in China. Tellingly, this is where the venerable Chateau Lafite Rothschild elected to launch their joint enterprise with the Citic Group, a nationalized Chinese investment group. It is also noteworthy to mention that the nation's largest producer, the China Great Wall Wine Company, is located within the region.[126]

Hebei Province

The Hebei Province is adjacent to the Shandong Province and its orientation to the Yellow Sea and Bohai Bay allows for a mild climate that can also support European grapes. The result is that it is the second most prolific province in the country, specializing in both dry whites and reds. However, the most famous wine from the region may be wines that are traditionally produced by longyan grapes (known as Dragon's Eyes), a type of grape that actually belongs to *Vitis vinifera*. This grape varietal is sometimes confused with Longan fruit, a lychee-like fruit that is grown in the south of China. The grape has been used by the Great Wall Wine Company to make white wine since the 1970s.[127]

---

[126] MacNeil, *The Wine Bible*, 913.

[127] Ibid, 913.

Beijing

The capital is officially a "direct controlled" municipality and is located within the Hebei Province. The climate, which tends to be dry and gets plenty of sunshine in the summer months, would be a prolific region, if there were more room for cultivation. However, there is still a number of important producers including Dragon Seal and Fengshou Wine Co.[128]

In the city of Beijing, there is a blossoming wine industry that has something for every wine enthusiast. *The Grape Wall of China* is the premier English language blog on Chinese wine, operated from Beijing by Jim Boyce. The blog is an excellent resource on the Chinese wine industry and hosts a number of live events, including "The China Wine Tour" which features a visit to four bars and samples of eight Chinese wines. This tour is a great offline adjunct experience to have along with the popular blog. There are also annual events including "The Grape Wall Challenge" where Chinese consumers vote on their favorite wines.

Tianjin

This interesting region is located about an hour from Beijing on the Bohai Gulf. The Bohai is the most interior bay of the Yellow Sea and the closest port to the capital city. As a result, it is an easy place to make a day trip from Beijing.

---

[128] Ibid, 913.

It is the fifth largest city in mainland China, offering a rich cultural heritage, forged as a port city that was influenced by foreigners engaged in commerce, many of whom eventually settled there. It boasts a unique cuisine that centers around the abundance of seafood available. Additionally, there are other interesting aspects such as a vibrant stand-up comedy scene that has produced some of China's most famous comics.

Given its rich cultural heritage which was influenced by foreigners, it is fitting that it was the site chosen for the founding of Dynasty Wines. Dynasty was an agreement between Tianjin and Remy Martin in 1980. It was one of the early sino-foreign ventures. Today, Dynasty is one of China's Big Three wineries along with Changyu and Great Wall.

Aside from the historic partnership that created Dynasty, there is not a lot to see with regards to the industry in Tianjin, so, most wine tourists would be better off exploring other regions. However, it is a bustling city with much to see and experience.

Liaoning Province

The location and climate of the Liaoning Province has allowed it to gain attention for ice wines that are derived from Vidal grapes. The province is also the industrial center of China, and as a result the industries that are heavily involved in the production of energy from fossil fuels create a milieu that may not make for the most appetizing atmosphere for producing world class wines.

Jilin Province

The region is home to *Vitis amurensis*, an indigenous varietal that is hardy enough to withstand extremely cold temperatures. This has inspired local scientists to try to use it in creating a hybrid by crossing it with certain types of *Vitis vinifera* to create desirable grapes that can withstand frigid conditions.[129]

The region has been making wine for over a century, making it an important stop for those who want to get a feel for how the wine industry has developed in China and for those who are interested in the innovation that produced *Vitis amurensis*.

Shanxi Province

The boutique wineries in this region are all situated within the Taiyuan Basin. This region would not be noteworthy had it not been where the Grace Vineyard had been founded in 1997.

The origin of Grace Vineyard is also an interesting tale of family, innovation, and, of course, wine. Chun-Keung Chan was a magnate based in Hong Kong who made a great deal of money in several fields, including the development of infrastructure and utilities, corporate investment, and real estate. He traveled widely for his work, and his time in France exposed him to the wine industry. As he became more in love with wine and more intrigued with wine making, he wondered why China didn't produce the fine wines that so many other countries did.

---

[129] Ibid, 913.

This question began a quest for the right place to grow wine in China, which led him to Taigu County in Shanxi where he decided to found Grace Vineyard. When some questioned his decision to open a vineyard in a province known for coal-mining and the collateral pollution from the industry, his response was twofold. First, he had worked in the coal industry in Shanxi a few decades earlier, and he was struck by how the industry was despoiling such a beautiful environment. Grace was a way for him to combat the deleterious effects of the coal industry in the region. Second, while searching for a location to put his vineyard, he discovered that the soil in Shanxi drained similarly to Bordeaux, giving him an ideal place to pursue cultivation of the noble grape. So, he started Grace Vineyard with the idea that it could be a natural oasis in Shanxi and perhaps encourage others to pursue more natural ventures in contrast with the coal industry. The name Grace reflects his sensibilities, especially when one considers its Chinese name Yi Yuan, which means "Elegant and Beautiful Garden."[130]

In creating his garden, Chun-Keung Chan had the foresight to consider the future for his family. As a result, he gave the reins of the vineyard to his daughter, Judy Chan, at the tender age of 24. Judy, an alumnus of the University of Michigan, stepped right in and proved savvy. Under her leadership, the vineyard gained a reputation as making some of the finest wine in China. Acclaim would follow, including nods of approval from some of the biggest names in the international wine scene including Jancis Robinson and *Wine Spectator*. Today, Grace Vineyard is regularly

---

[130] "Grace Vineyard," accessed June 27, 2018, http://en.grace-vineyard.com/.

mentioned as one of the finest vineyards in China and is worth a visit simply to witness its beauty and to taste premium Chinese wine.

Additionally, Chateau Rongzi, founded in 2007, became immediately notable after Jean-Claude Berrouet was hired to be the vineyard's consultant. He came to prominence as the vintner for Chateau Petrus, a world-famous Bordeaux vineyard that produces one of the most sought-after wines in the world; it is especially popular in China. Although this winery is overshadowed by Grace, they are producing wine that continues to turn heads.

Ningxia Hui Autonomous Region

The Ningxia Hui Autonomous Region lies about five hundred miles west of Beijing. For oenophiles, it is worth the trip from the capital because more than fifty wineries are rapidly expanding production there. If you're planning to visit a region of China specifically for a wine experience, you may be best served by heading to the Ningxia Hui. Known to many Chinese as "the Napa Valley of China," this region is nourished by the Yellow River which provides irrigation to the dry climate to produce an excellent setting for grape cultivation and appreciation. As a result, both the government and private investors have poured money into the region, making Ningxia (the short name for the region) the premier destination. This is where Louis Vuitton Moet Hennessy (LVMH) chose to open Chandon China, the nation's first sparkling wine house. The winery is a joint venture with a Chinese company which invested a total of $28 million in the project with LVMH. Karen McNeil, author of *The Wine*

Bible, has spent a great deal of time in China and asserts that the creation of Chandon portends great things, not only for the future of Ningxia, but the entire wine industry in the country as a whole. McNeil, speaking of the investment by LVMH, stated, "To spend this kind of money here is a thumbs-up in terms of its confidence in the Chinese market."[131]

The region is a microcosm of what makes the modern Chinese wine industry so special. Without large pools of tractable labor, the wine industry in Ningxia would not survive, much less thrive. Although the hot temperatures make the region a hospitable climate for wine grapes during the growing season, stiff winds blow down from Siberia in the winter, causing freezing temperatures that plummet well below zero degrees Fahrenheit. This is a major contributing factor to why *Vitis vinifera* historically never made it there and in much of northern China. But trial and error, along with sheer determination, has produced a workable strategy that has allowed *Vitis vinifera* to flourish in Ningxia. A central part of this strategy is utilizing the practice of burying vines every winter to protect them from the bitter cold and then unearthing them every spring and reforming them into canopies. The work is difficult and labor intensive; without the large pools of inexpensive laborers, this would not be possible.[132]

---

[131] "China Makes Big Bet on Turning Desert into Wine Region," CBS News, January 1, 2016, https://www.cbsnews.com/news/china-aims-become-top-wine-producer-ningxia-region-vineyards/.

[132] Mustacich, *Thirsty Dragon*, 65.

However, there is an even bigger long-term obstacle for the grape industry in Ningxia: desertification. This problem is not limited to Nangxia, as more than 25% of China is affected by desertification. In the words of Zhang Yongli, deputy director of China's State Forestry Administration, "Land desertification is the most important ecological problem in China."[133]

Interestingly, the wine industry in Ningxia is unfazed by these seemingly massive problems. Today, there are more than 80,000 acres of vineyards planted in Ningxia, and by 2020 there are plans to have more than 160,000 acres. To put this in perspective, this would be about three times the quantity produced in Napa Valley. The robust output in Napa Valley, which has an ideal climate for many varieties of grapes, took about a century to cultivate; in Ningxia, about a decade was enough to do so. This is cultivation on a grand scale that is unprecedented in the history of wine making.[134]

Li Jianhua, party head of Ningxia, stated in an interview with China Daily: "By 2020, we will build the region into the wine capital of the East with more than one hundred quality wineries." He predicted that "This will generate 100 billion yuan ($15.7 billion) in revenue and 100,000 jobs."[135]

If there is one vineyard not to miss while visiting Ningxia, it would be Silver Heights. Founded by Lin Gao in 1999, the vineyard has some

---

[133] Mustacich, *Thirsty Dragon*, 94.

[134] "China Makes Big Bet on Turning Desert into Wine Region", 2.

[135] Friefelder and Jibu, "Wine in the US: 'Made in China' Is Rare."

striking similarities to Grace Vineyards in that the vineyards both prize quality over quantity and that they are family affairs. Silver Heights' wine maker is founder Lin Gao's daughter Emma, who many industry insiders consider to be the best native winemaker in China. Emma learned the ins and outs of winery management and vinting in France, and the evidence of her knowledge and abilities can be found in every bottle of Silver Heights.

Gansu Province

While visiting Ningxia, you can easily stop over to the Gansu Province, which boasts a cooler climate conducive to producing other varieties of grapes. Given that it is cooler and there is a shorter season, late-harvest grapes, more suitable to the weather, tend to do well. On its own, Gansu is not a good wine destination, so it is recommended as a coda for itineraries to other more prolific regions.

Inner Mongolia

Inner Mongolia has a rich history of grape cultivation. During the brief growing season, the weather is suitable for cultivation, however the winters can be brutal. The arid winters are frigid and without snow cover; the ground becomes hard and freezes deeply. This condition has made the area into the premier place to explore techniques for cold weather cultivation and to try out varieties that can withstand the brutalities of the extreme climate. Like the Jilin Province, there have been efforts to make hybrids from the native *Vitis amurensis* and *Vitis vinifera*, with varying degrees of success. The successful crosses have been given simple, humble names such as "Red Wine Grape #1."

The most interesting *Vitis vinifera* is referred to as Tuo Xian, is pinkish in color, and occurs in large luscious bunches. The grape is used in a sweet white wine that is combined with flowers from the bushy *Osmanthus fragrans* to produce a fragrant dessert wine that is famous in China.

Inner Mongolia is an excellent destination for those with a sense of adventure. Not only will adventurers enjoy the unique terrain, but they'll also have the opportunity to try wine from grape varieties that are unavailable outside of the region, much less China.

Xinjiang Uyghur Autonomous Region

The Xinjiang Uyghur Autonomous region is perhaps the most unique cultural crossroads in China. Visitors can pair their wines with kebabs and listen to the sweet sounds of a *muezzin* calling other muslims to prayer. Visitors can watch the sunset as a backdrop on the minarets of a mosque, while sampling local reds.

Jancis Robinson was impressed by some of the wines in the region. On her blog, she wrote, "Lou Lan Cabernet 1999 had been by far the most impressive wine I had tasted on my first brief visit to China in January 2002."[136]

---

[136] Jancis Robinson, "My Chinese Adventures - Part II," Jancis Robinson, February 1, 2004, https://www.jancisrobinson.com/articles/my-chinese-adventures-part-ii.

Northern Xinjiang, like other wine regions in northern China, has to contend with the frigid gusts of wind that come down from Siberia. Robinson observed how the viticulturist must deal with the cold every fall: "Vine canes have to be bent horizontal and covered by long mounds of the soft, sandy, loamy soils typical of most Chinese vineyards which in summer are carefully re-shaped so as to provide irrigation channels."[137]

Yunnan Province and Sichuan Province

Many of those who have carefully scrutinized the varied terrains and climates of China think this region may have the best potential to produce the best wine in China. Being near Tibet in Western China, it has a high elevation. Sichuan has two distinct regions, the fertile Sichuan Basin on the eastern side and the western portion which is on the eastern part of the Tibet Plateau (often referred to as Qinghai-Tibet Plateau in China). Yunnan is also a mountainous region with an average elevation near 2,000 meters (over a mile high). As a result, the regions have a high elevation that allows for a great deal of sun, helping to properly mature the grapes.

However, the mountains make it hard to secure large swaths of land for cultivation, so the vineyards in these provinces tend to be a bit spread out. This should not deter the traveler from visiting this region because there are so many great aspects, from unique cultural

---

[137] Ibid.

opportunities to outstanding cuisine. This is bolstered by the fact that within these regions lies arguably the best opportunity to cultivate the finest grapes in China.

CHAPTER IX

The Future of the Chinese Wine Industry

How the 2012 Crackdown has Changed the Chinese Wine Market

As we had established before, graft and conspicuous consumption became hallmarks of how the upper-level Chinese officials conducted business. These shows of wealth—lavish parties at five-star hotels, Rolex watches as gifts, and toasts with Bordeaux's finest reds—came under increasing scrutiny as billions of poor Chinese starved in the countryside. This came to a head in the high profile trial of Politburo, member of the Communist Party, and Communist Party Secretary, Bo Xilai, for abuse of power and corruption, including bribery. The plot thickened as Bo's wife was accused of murdering English businessman Neil Heywood. Gu Kail was convicted in July of poisoning Heywood, creating a public drama that reached the very heart of power in China.

As a result of mounting pressure to right the ship for the Communist Party of China, Xi Jinping, who took control of China from Chairman Hu Jintao in November 2012, enacted a thorough anti-corruption campaign against "tigers and flies" (in other words senior officials and mid- and lower-ranking officials respectively). Heads would roll. In the next eighteen months, almost 250,000 were either detained or charged as a result. While in custody, seventy died, some of whom committed suicide. This was followed by a flurry of activity in the upper echelons of Chinese society to hide money overseas.[138]

These developments at the top of Chinese society had far-reaching consequences which affected the wine industry. Logically, one would think that only the big-ticket French imports would decline as a result of the anti-corruption campaign. The impact in 2013 was minimal, perhaps due to the infancy of the campaign. However, the 2014 statistics revealed the huge hole in the industry with exports to China and Hong Kong falling 9 percent in volume and seventeen percent in value. [139]

The deputy director-general of the Federation of Exporters of Wines and Spirits of France (CFTS), Pierre Genest, stated, "This is clearly the fight against extravagance announced in early 2013, which impacted the products with higher added value and the older

---

[138] Diane Francis, "China's Anti-Corruption Crackdown Threatens to Spill over into Canada," *Financial Post*, August 8, 2014, https://business.financialpost.com/opinion/chinas-anti-corruption-crackdown-threatens-to-spill-over-into-canada.

[139] Agence France-Presse, "Chinese Corruption Crackdown, Bad Harvest Leads to Bordeaux Wine Sales Fall," *The Guardian*, March 20, 2015, sec. World news, http://www.theguardian.com/world/2015/mar/20/chinese-corruption-crackdown-bad-harvest-leads-to-bordeaux-wine-sales-fall.

Cognacs and wines of Bordeaux."[140] The fact that imports, such as expensive Bordeaux, dropped precipitously in 2014 is no surprise; what is surprising is the impact that the crackdown had on the entire Chinese market.

"The slump in government orders in 2013, which I witnessed first-hand at Treaty Port," Chris Ruffle recollects in *A Decent Bottle of Wine in China*, "was reflected not only in the economic performance of other winemakers, but in the performance of almost all luxury items. This illustrates the important role which gift-giving plays in Chinese society in general, and the wine business in particular."[141]

Although wine was among many markets hit hard by the crackdowns, the situation is not dire for the wine industry. Most commentators see the industry's potential for growth to far outweigh any political or climate-related problems. All indications point to the consumption of wine in China growing, as will production.[142] This period will be seen, with more hindsight, as a bump in the road and the industry will continue to grow due to the Millennials, rising middle class, and domestic production among other factors.

---

[140] Agence France-Presse, "China's Anti-Bling Push Hits French Wine Exports," *Wine-Searcher*, September 10, 2014, https://www.wine-searcher.com/m/2014/09/china-s-anti-bling-push-hits-french-wine-exports.

[141] Ruffle, *A Decent Bottle of Wine in China*, 151.

[142] See Figures 1 and 2 in Appendix.

Electronic and Mobile Commerce May Define the Future of Chinese Wine Consumption

A new batch of wine lovers seemingly pushing the trend are more enamored with the New World wines. Successful young Chinese in their twenties and thirties see the choice of wine as an aspect of their worldly sophistication. Increasingly, they are using electronic devices to learn about, compare, and purchase wine. In 2013, it was estimated that 27 percent of all wine purchased in China was done via the internet.[143] Contrasting this with European purchases at 8 to 10 percent and the United States where only 2 percent of the population bought wine over the web.[144] A study in 2014 found that 47 percent of consumers surveyed said they had purchased wine through the internet in the past six months.[145]

When compared with the rest of the world, China is far ahead in Internet wine purchases. This trend has had some interesting aspects including digital tastings, where wine is shipped by producers to Chinese wine experts in Shanghai where they log on to Skype and enjoy the wine with the direction of the producers who can be located anywhere in the

---

[143] Todd Balazovic, "Wine Growers Go Online to Boost Sales," *China Daily Europe*, March 7, 2014, http://europe.chinadaily.com.cn/epaper/2014-03/07/content_17329583.htm.

[144] Ibid.

[145] Lauren Eads, "China's Taste for Imported Wines Doubles," *The Drinks Business* (blog), June 30, 2014, https://www.thedrinksbusiness.com/2014/06/chinas-taste-for-imported-wines-doubles/.

world. The internet has offered a way for smaller producers around the world to get a presence in China without having to shell out the expensive travel costs, instead using an internet connection.[146]

China has also become the largest e-commerce market on the planet, passing the United States. In a 2014 study, it was revealed that 62 percent of Chinese shop online weekly, compared to an average of 21 percent across the rest of the globe. Mobile commerce is becoming a large part of how the Chinese have chosen to acquire their goods. In 2013, mobile commerce increased by 169 percent as China continued to move in the direction of being a consumer society.[147]

In the words of wine blogger about China, Jim Boyce, "Chinese consumers are very sophisticated. They are armed with smartphones now."[148] Although there are impediments—including internet access, connectivity, and inadequate product information—there are signs that perhaps mobile commerce will be another major contributor to the expansion of electronic wine commerce and the wine industry as a whole. In a field survey of Chinese visitors in the UK, conducted by the Consilience Group, results showed that 70 percent of those questioned believed that a wine app would be useful. Akalin and Lazar published a thorough study of electronic and mobile commerce as it relates to the wine industry in China. What they found is that the "technology is still

---

[146] Balazovic, "Wine Growers Go Online to Boost Sales."

[147] Akalin and Lazar, *Wine in China*, location 267.

[148] Balazovic, "Wine Growers Go Online to Boost Sales."

in its early stages and has not caught on in the wine industry, but will become more popular in the future."[149]

The speed at which technology changed the wine industry was fast. A year after Akalin and Lazar looked into the industry, some of its leaders met at Vinexpo Hong Kong's 2016 special China Market Conference to discuss the state of the industry and specifically the role of technology as a change agent. There Chris Tung, Chief Marketing Officer of Alibaba, asserted, "Physical distribution channels can be complex, but people have developed a steady habit for buying online, which now accounts for 30 percent of all consumer sales in China." He then stated, "In five years' time, we expect sales of alcoholic products on various online platforms to account for about 70 percent of total wine and spirits sales in China."[150]

Many producers feel that they have an uphill battle to compete with traditional producers like France who export high volumes to China. Due to poor offerings from major producers early on in China, and also to the stigma from the many fake wines produced, there is a special trust that Chinese have with certain foreign brands. Social media and other eCommerce tools are being utilized by Chinese producers to cultivate fans in China. As Judy Chan, co-owner of Grace Vineyard, which is noted for producing premium wines, suggested, "We have to

---

[149] Akalin and Lazar, *Wine in China*, location 348-363.

[150] Vinexpo Newsroom, "E-Commerce to Drive Triple Growth for Wine in China," *Vinexpo Newsroom - Wine & Spirits News by Vinexpo* (blog), June 3, 2016, https://www.vinexpo-newsroom.com/e-commerce-to-drive-triple-growth-for-wine-in-china/.

find ways to connect with the consumers. In China, personal connections are important, so we do intimate 'personalised' events with direct consumer interaction." This can be done cheaply and easily online compared to other traditional marketing strategies. So what does that mean as far as marketing strategies?[151]

"Consumers buy from people or dealers they know. Consumers need that wine experience, to know and feel the story of the brands. But consumers in China don't always know where to go, so big brands are guiding consumers, for instance through wine education to help them switch from easy and cheap wines to more valuable wines," said Xavier Pignel-Dupont, Greater China–Asia Pacific Director of Castel Frères SAS. Ultimately, "Branding strategies will evolve in China, and the focus will be much more on the brand story," observed Robert Foye, Managing Director of Australia's Treasury Wine Estates.[152]

"It's a big, messy and grey market, so we need to bring brands in for value. We believe eCommerce will offer strong new channels for sales, so we're investing big in education and visibility, as we see a big growth in digital," stated Frantz Hotton, Managing Director of Pernod Ricard Hong Kong & Macau. No matter the difference in opinion on certain aspects of how to use eCommerce to sell wine in China, it is clear that the experts agree that it is a major force in the

---

[151] Ibid.

[152] Ibid.

market that will continue to transform how people do business in the Chinese wine industry.[153]

How Good are Chinese Wines?

China burst onto the international scene with Helan Qing Xue Jia Bei Lan 2009. This red was produced in the Bordeaux style by blending merlot, cabernet sauvignon, and carménère (often referred to as Cabernet Gernischt in China). The wine was crowned the best Red Bordeaux Varietal during the 2011 Decanter World Wine Awards. This wine received global attention as the first Chinese wine to win an international award, and the price tag of about twenty dollars made it an excellent place for oenophiles to begin their exploration of Chinese reds. However, with only about 13,000 bottles produced, it may be hard to get your hands on a bottle, especially at original market price.

Jim Boyce reflects that, "While there are several dozen producers making decent wines now, the prices are quite high by international standards." [154] The high prices for quality wine combined with the domestic demand for wine make the export of Chinese wine a rarity. In 2015, Karl Storchmann, an economist at New York University and editor of the Journal of Wine Economics, stated that China "will need a few flagship brands to be able to compete at the high end."[155]

---

[153] Ibid.

[154] FlorCruz, "China's Wine Industry Explodes, But Not Yet On The World Stage."

[155] Ibid.

Although the Helan Qing Xue Jia Bei La was the first to bring international attention to the quality Chinese wine, there are several wineries emerging on the high end that will transform China's future. Two that seem to be spearheading the quality are boutique vineyards that make world-class wine. They are Silver Heights and Grace Vineyard.

Emma Gao is a truly outstanding winemaker. The story is now legendary of how she founded the Silver Heights winery with the help of her father, Gao Lin. After Gao Lin lost his job as the general manager of a government-run clothing factory in Yinchuan, the capital of the Ningxia Hui Autonomous region, due to a sudden closure, he had to scramble to find work. In 1992, his two brothers founded an export company with him in St. Petersburg. He moved to Russia with his oldest daughter, Emma, who studied economics at Saint Petersburg University.[156]

He returned to work for a chemical factory outside of Yinchuan in 1997 when Emma had completed her university studies. The next year, Gao Lin was assigned to work on an 823-acre farm where they wanted to grow grapes. In 1999, Gao Lin went on a junket to Germany and France to study the cultivation and appreciation of wine grapes, along with other related aspects of wine tourism. He returned with a passion for wine and it took little convincing for his daughter Emma to accept his offer to study the wine industry in Bordeaux, enrolling in a three-year course. She excelled in her studies and when she returned, the seed was planted for them to get serious about their own family winery

---

[156] Mustacich, *Thirsty Dragon*, 53-56.

where they intended to produce world-class wines. They called it Silver Heights, producing their first vintage in 2007 and from the first taste, it was clear that Emma Gao had a special talent for making wine.[157]

Emma Gao is still doing great things at Silver Heights. In the words of wine maven Jancis Robinson, who has met outstanding vintners all over the world: "I honestly think that Emma Gao, despite the obvious paucity of financial backing, is the most naturally vivacious wine producer I have ever met." She makes some great wine.[158]

Silver Heights Emma's Reserve 2011 is probably her best offering. Savoring a sample of this wine is the best way to taste the results of the height of her creative powers. But the wine is certainly not cheap, retailing for about $200 per bottle. If you are going to splurge to find out how good Chinese wine is, this is probably the wine to try. The wine is ninety percent Cabernet Sauvignon with the balance being carménère. It has deep red fruit and is smooth.

You can sample a premium wine from Grace at a fraction of the cost of Emma's Reserve: Grace Vineyard Deep Blue 2010. The wine is interesting because it gets its body and more broadly the structure from Cabernet Sauvignon (74%) and is softened by Merlot (21%), while adding 5% Cabernet France, giving the wine deeper complexity. The wine highlights dark fruit with balanced tannins. You can get your hands on a bottle for around forty dollars.

---

[157] Ibid, 64-72.

[158] Jancis Robinson, "Emma Gao - a Story of Wine Today," Jancis Robinson, November 29, 2012, https://www.jancisrobinson.com/articles/emma-gao-a-story-of-wine-today.

If sparkling wine is your thing, Grace Vineyards has something special to try. Grace Vineyards, known for producing some of the finest wines in China, is one of the most recognizable names in the Chinese wine scene. After six years of careful preparation, they unveiled their "Angelina" sparkling wine series in 2015. Nearly all critics agree that everything that Grace Vineyard does is tasteful and well thought out. Commenting on their line of sparkling wine, owner Judy Chan said, "I am obsessed with all kinds of bubbles. Ten years ago I had the idea in my mind to make a beautiful sparkling wine."[159] Indeed, she made several of them. They have carefully crafted three sparkling wines that each feature a single grape varietal: Chennin Blanc, Cabernet Franc, and Cabernet Sauvignon. They also feature their 2009 Brut Reserve, which is made exclusively from Chardonnay. This wine has been acclaimed by critics.

Titans in the Wine Industry Turn their Attention to China

Jancis Robinson and Robert M. Parker Jr. are two of the most influential wine commentators in the world. They have both realized the importance of the Chinese wine industry and its changing place in the world wine scene, now more complex and varied than any other

---

[159] Glass of Bubbly, "Angelina, New Sparkling Wine from Grace Vineyard in China," *Glass Of Bubbly* (blog), August 28, 2015, https://www.glassofbubbly.com/angelina-new-sparkling-wine-from-grace-vineyard-in-china/.

time in history. As critic Michael Broadbent wrote in *Decanter* magazine, "My feeling is that consumers have never had so much choice, but they have never been so confused. The whole world is making a good standard of wine today, and they need some guidance."[160] Although Broadbent might not have had Chinese wine in mind when he made these comments, they apply to the Chinese wine industry with increasing importance as it continues to expand and as more Chinese wine is exported.

Jancis Robinson was the first woman to earn the title Master of Wine and has a celebrity status in England. Moreover, she has a great deal of sway in the international wine scene. She has made multiple trips to China, chronicling them on her website, for *The Financial Times*, and in *The World of Wine 7th Edition* which she co-wrote with Hugh Johnson. She has been an outspoken critic of those who contend that wine tasting can be completely objective. She acknowledges that people have different preferences and tastes. She has also suggested that certain tasting notes are culturally biased. One glaring example of this, she contends, is that certain fruits, regularly described by the Western palate, do not exist in other important parts of the world. As she points out: "A sizeable portion of flavors (particularly fruits) described in standard wine texts are simply unknown to the Chinese."[161]

In 2002, Robinson was briefly in China, when she sampled several wines that interested her and was apparently so enchanted with what

---

[160] Quoted in Taber, *A Toast to Bargain Wines*, 72.

[161] Quoted in Taber, *A Toast to Bargain Wines*, 39-40.

she found that she returned for a more extensive trip in 2004. After seeing the scale of the production in the growing vineyards of China she reflected, "When the Chinese decide to do something, their efficiency and single-mindedness is only just this side of terrifying." She was struck by the tendency of farmers to produce the highest yield possible, something natural in a nation of more than a billion people. Robinson observed that when applied to viticulture, "The tendency…leads to too many leaves and not enough ripe fruit." This was in line with many critics who found Chinese wines around the turn of the twenty-first century to be somewhat thin and grassy-tasting, which are signs that the cultivation of the fruit has been stretched too far. She noted at the time: "The great mass of the population find it too expensive relative to beer even to contemplate. The middle classes know that wine is officially approved of and is the height of fashion but do not necessarily like its taste. Stories of diluting wine with cola and lemonade are legion." However, she did find many wines she enjoyed on her second trip and concluded: "It will be some time before China has any significant quantity of wine of serious interest to the rest of the world (although given Chinese determination, that time could be much shorter than I imagine)." She seemed taken and would continue to write about wine in China.[162]

Ever since her first visit, she would continue to travel to China every couple years, and she would try to visit a different region and try new wines. Robinson wrote that in the first decade in the new millennium,

---

[162] Robinson, "My Chinese Adventures - Part II."

she did not see much of an elevation in quality as the quantity churned out rapidly expanded. However, in 2014 she attended a blind tasting of fifty-three wines in Shanghai, which she said "represented a snapshot of where Chinese wine has got to." After tasting the wines, she found several reds that impressed her and that she greatly enjoyed. However, of all the whites, there was only one that she "would drink with any pleasure." So what was the upshot? "The number of good Chinese wines is definitely rising fast. This range would have been unthinkable ten years ago. France, watch out."[163]

In March of 2016, Robinson made another pass through China. She tasted a number of fine New World wines with leading Chinese wine enthusiasts. She said little about actual Chinese wine, but said a great deal about how wine appreciation was changing in China in these two sentences: "I saw very strong signs of the diversification of the Chinese wine market. In fact I hardly saw a bottle of red Bordeaux." This observation is referring to the fact that at one time Bordeaux dominated the Chinese import market, but through wine education and recognition, Chinese wine drinkers have opened their eyes to many types of wine from countries other than France. This can also refer to the new options available within China from domestic production. Through her travels in China, over the course of time, she witnessed the rapid transformation of the wine industry and wine consumption.[164]

---

[163] Jancis Robinson, "Chinese Wine - Catching up Fast," Jancis Robinson, April 5, 2014, https://www.jancisrobinson.com/articles/chinese-wine-catching-up-fast.

[164] Jancis Robinson, "Kiwi Wines Please Chinese Palates," Jancis Robinson, March 7, 2016, https://www.jancisrobinson.com/articles/kiwi-wines-please-chinese-palates.

Robinson's famous palate is certainly leading the West's forays into the burgeoning wine industry in China. Her U.S. counterpart, Robert Parker, arguably the world's most famous wine critic, is certainly behind Robinson in his exploration of the Chinese wine industry. But, he still has made his mark on the Chinese wine scene.

Robert M. Parker Jr. tends to like bolder and richer wines than Robinson, observed leading wine journalist George M. Taber. After earning a degree in law, Parker rose to prominence through his publication called *The Wine Advocate*. He went on to create the one hundred point scale for scoring wines. He embarked upon a dazzling career, penning best-sellers about wine and his 2005 biography by Elin McCoy was entitled: *The Emperor of Wine*. This title described his vast clout, something not lost on the Chinese. His presence in China showed that it had arrived on the international wine scene, especially in the U.S. where Parker is one of the most influential wine critics. In May of 2008, Parker selected the wines for a seven-course dinner with wine pairings for the equivalent of $2,300. There were several exquisite French wines including: Louis Jadot Corton-Charlemagne Grand Cru 2002 and E. Guigal Côte-Rôtie La Turque 1999, but Chinese wine was conspicuously absent. The event was held with all the pomp one would expect, on top of The Great Wall of China. Jim Boyce—who runs the well-respected *Grape Wall of China*, perhaps the best wine blog in China—attended the event. Boyce artfully captured the moment on his blog: "Watchtowers lit in gold, walkways lit in silver—the Great Wall shone like an ornate necklace draped over a mountain of wrinkled black velvet. Long-silenced iron cannons pointed at the ghosts of invading hordes, white flags cracked in the cool stiff breeze. The moon hung low, orange as a ripe gourd." From the way Boyce recounts the event, it was dazzling, and Parker did not disappoint. Most guests were, however, disappointed not to spend some time with the visiting wine expert. As Boyce noted: "Like 80 percent of the attendees, I was at one of the other four tables. I can't help but think that had Parker spent a course at each table, we would have been happier and he would have learned a great deal about the China wine market."[165]

Parker held a question-and-answer session a couple days after the tasting, which Boyce also attended. He asked Parker point blank about Chinese wine and Parker responded that he had not had the time and pleasure to try the wine, but added that he was anxious to try some Chinese wine that afternoon. When asked about his impressions of the Chinese wine industry, he said that he believed that the quality would increase with each passing year, citing the emergence of the U.S. wine industry as an example of increased growth of quantity and quality. He concluded the session with this interesting opinion: "China is well ahead of where the U.S. was thirty years ago. A lot of Americans in my generation traveled to Europe and got interested in wine. Here, you are

---

[165] Jim Boyce, "Beijing Bob: Dinner with Robert Parker on the Great Wall of China," *Grape Wall of China*, June 6, 2008, http://www.grapewallofchina.com/2008/06/06/robert-parker-wine-dinner-china/.

moving much faster," Parker reflected and then added: "I want to play a part. I want to show my passion for wine."[166]

Parker revisited China in early 2014 for an additional tasting. In December of 2015, *Robert Parker Wine Advocate* and *RobertParker.com*, "the world's most widely read independent consumer's guide to fine wine," made an important announcement that reflected the growing importance of China. Liwen Hao, wine educator and wine writer, was hired to be their Asian Wine Reviewer. He will be based in Shanghai and do his reporting for *Robert Parker Wine Advocate*. When asked about the new position, Liwen Hao said that it was an honor, adding: "I feel that China and other areas are coming of age in terms of grape growing and winemaking. It is my hope to bring many high quality, truly interesting Asian wines to the attention of the wine world."[167]

Parker and Robinson have made names for themselves in the global wine community by doing tireless research to spot trends, and stay ahead of the pack of critics vying for the top of the mountain. The fact that both critics have been forced to pay attention to China is evidence that the wine industry of this sleeping dragon has awakened and can no longer be ignored in the global wine industry.

---

[166] Jim Boyce, "Wine Word - Robert Parker in Beijing," *Grape Wall of China*, May 27, 2008, http://www.grapewallofchina.com/2008/05/27/robert-parker-beijing-china-wine-tasting/.

[167] "Robert Parker Wine Advocate Announces: New Reviewer In China And New Office In Napa," Charles Communications Associates, December 17, 2015, http://www.charlescomm.com/Big-News/robert-parker-wine-advocate-announces--new-reviewer-in-china-and-new-office-in-napa.html.

The Future and Hong Kong

The luxury auction houses, Christie's and Sotheby's, have started holding regular wine auctions in Hong Kong after the island eliminated its duties on wine in 2008. By 2009, Hong Kong had already become the most important wine center for Sotheby's, even more so than established hubs like London and New York City.[168] On the island of Hong Kong in 2013, Acker Merrall & Condit, the premier auction house for wine, broke 483 world records for money paid for wine.[169]

Due to over-planting in the 1990s, there was a glut of wine worldwide around the turn of the century. The OIV reported that in 2009 global consumption was exceeded by about 359 million cases of wine.[170]

On October 22, 2013 Morgan Stanley released a report entitled, "The Global Wine Industry: Slowly moving from balance to shortage." This report sounded the alarm that a global wine shortage was underway that sent shockwaves throughout the wine community. The report explained that after there was a glut of wine to the tune of 600 million cases in 2004, in 2012 demand exceeded supply. After production peaked in 2004, it steadily declined. According to the report, "Production in 2012 also fell to its lowest levels in more than

---

[168] Malcolm Moore, "Hong Kong Becomes World's Largest Wine Market," *The Daily Telegraph*, October 6, 2009, sec. Food and Drink, https://www.telegraph.co.uk/foodanddrink/wine/6264679/Hong-Kong-becomes-worlds-largest-wine-market.html.

[169] MacNeil, *The Wine Bible*, 909.

[170] Taber, *A Toast to Bargain Wines*, 23.

forty years." In the meantime, consumption jumped in 2010 and continued to grow. They projected that this would cause a spike in price as demand would continue to outpace supply. One of the major factors in the new trend was: growing consumption in China.[171]

In fact, wine consumption in China doubled twice between 2008 and 2013.[172] Moreover, China became the world's number one consumer of red wine at the end of 2013, emptying 155 million nine-liter cases and out-drinking the French and Italians at 150 million and 141 million respectively. The expansion of the market in the first decade of the twenty-first century was massive and then there is the question of how to supply the market.[173]

The majority of China's wine consumption comes from domestic production, over 80 percent.[174] Domestic production has expanded rapidly to quench the expanding thirst of Chinese consumers. Rising wine appreciation from experience and formal education could be the most important factor in the equation of the many factors driving the increase in consumption.

In fact, this is something that Chris Ruffle addresses in his book, *A Decent Bottle of Wine In China*. He adds nuance to the discussion of factors leading to increased consumption in China. Speaking from a

---

[171] "The Global Wine Industry" (New York NY.: Morgan Stanley Research, October 22, 2013), http://gavinquinney.com/wp-content/uploads/2013/11/MS_wine.pdf, 1.

[172] Ibid, 56.

[173] Chow, "China Is Now World's Biggest Consumer of Red Wine.", 1-2.

[174] Ibid, 2.

wealth of first-hand experience, he points out: "With growing wealth and travel, the wine drinkers of China are starting to understand what good wine should taste like, and which wines best suit Chinese dishes." Ruffle sees that the various food and fake wine scandals have made Chinese consumers wary about ersatz products and therefore prize reliable and trustworthy products. This is forcing the big producers to make better wine and continues to expand the market for wines from little estate wineries like his own Treaty Port Vineyards, encouraging others to follow in their footsteps, the net result being more premium wine produced in China.[175]

In the decade leading up to the watershed year of 2013 when China became the largest consumer of red wine in the world, domestic production quadrupled.[176] Understanding this rapid development allows for deeper insight into the connection between consumption and production. For as production grows, there has been an increased production of domestically produced wine. However, these trends are best understood when viewed in relation to other global economic trends.

Although Morgan Stanley's report made it seem that wine was disappearing from the Earth, much of it going to warm the palates of Chinese wine lovers, this is not the whole story. The OIV reported that production was starting to rise again in late 2013 and consumption, worldwide, was stabilizing. In his book, *Wine Wars*,

---

[175] Ruffle, *A Decent Bottle of Wine in China*, 123.
[176] "The Global Wine Industry", 56.

Mike Veseth says that there was no reason for oenophiles to panic on the grounds that they're worried "they need to stock up on wine, because the Chinese are going to drink it all. I don't think that's going to happen." The larger issue is what he has referred to as the "China Syndrome" which he describes as "both the dream that China will buy all the goods we try to sell her and the fear that she will return the favor and take over our markets." Veseth's assertion, as we have seen in the course of this book, is that neither is completely true. But one thing is for sure, as he concisely put it, the Chinese "are on everybody's radar, either as an investment or as a market for exports." He sees a future where "the majority of wine China will drink...will be made in China." This may cause a different problem that Kharunya Paramaguru eloquently points out in her thoughtful article for *Time*, "How China Became the Wine World's Most Unlikely Superpower": "the real difficulty for wine lovers in the future could be in getting the chance to taste a bottle of Chinese red."[177]

We now know that China is the world's emerging superpower in the wine industry with both production and consumption increasing at unprecedented rates. But what does the future hold for the Chinese wine industry? There are many who believe that the market in China is starting to become saturated and that the growth in consumption cannot continue at the current pace. There are others who say that China cannot continue to grow its production because of a

---

[177] Kharunya Paramaguru, "How China Became the Wine World's Most Unlikely Superpower," *Time*, October 31, 2013, http://business.time.com/2013/10/31/how-china-became-the-wine-worlds-most-unlikely-superpower/, 1-2.

combination of factors. But the doubters are most likely wrong. For deeper insight into the future of the Chinese wine industry, it may be important to take a long look at Hong Kong.

Hong Kong has played a large role in the explosion of the Chinese wine industry because the traditional trading hub is not only strategically important for the import and export of wine, but it is also more wine-crazy than the mainland. After the British turned the island into one of the most prolific and important trading hubs in the world; it was returned to China in 1997. Although the island's sovereignty and relationship with the mainland has been complex and is beyond the scope of this book, its contribution to the ascent of the Chinese wine industry is vitally important. Anthony Mak, director of the Hong Kong Trade Development Council (HKTDC), had this to say about the relationship between the two: "On average, Chinese consumers are just consuming one-fifth of what Hong Kong consumers are doing [per capita] in terms of wine." These startling numbers show that there is a great potential for growth. Looking toward the future, Mak continued, "So even if China is the largest consumer market for wine in the world, it has a lot of potential to grow even further."[178]

We have established that the profile of wine drinkers in China is rapidly changing as wine increases in popularity. Recall that the earliest drinkers were wealthy Chinese, generally more interested in the label than the contents of the bottle. However, as education has exploded, so

---

[178] Jack Friefelder, "China's Wine Consumption Is Growing," *China Daily USA*, April 4, 2014, http://usa.chinadaily.com.cn/epaper/2014-04/25/content_17465188.htm.

has the variety of wine demanded by the newly interested consumer. As has been previously noted, part of this transition can be attributed to education as Chinese wine drinkers are becoming more sophisticated through self-education, the efforts of vineyards, and the tasting rooms in high-end liquor stores, bars, and restaurants that increasingly cater to wine consumers. Additionally, more than ever, a new generation consisting of Chinese students are studying at the premier schools for wine education in other countries. Three prominent examples are the Bordeaux International Wine Institute, the Burgundy Business School, and the Wine and Spirit Education Trust (WSET) in London. In China, as Chris Ruffle observes, "the thirst for wine education is unslakable."[179]

WSET was founded in 1969 and has grown rapidly since. Its courses are now offered in sixty countries and are available in eighteen languages. The school was given the Queen's Award for Enterprise in 2015 and in the academic year preceding that, 56,125 students across the globe took their internationally recognized qualifications (awards and diplomas earned from WSET courses). France has four times the number of students it had in 2008 taking the WSET requirements; Australians have increased their participation eight times in the same span of time. Although these increases are significant, China is close to overtaking the United Kingdom as WSET's top market.[180]

---

[179] Ruffle, *A Decent Bottle of Wine in China*, 153.

[180] Jancis Robinson, "Big Award for WSET," Jancis Robinson, April 21, 2015, https://www.jancisrobinson.com/articles/big-award-for-wset.

The Bordeaux International Wine Institute began in 2004 with twenty students eager to learn business management in the oenological arts. Today, the school has over one hundred students. As the school has grown, so has the presence of Chinese students. Aside from France, China has the largest number of students in the school, roughly thirty percent. This trend of Chinese studying wine in France is not limited to Bordeaux. The Burgundy Business School in Dijon has roughly a third of its students who study wine management hailing from China. This is a large increase from the span between 2009 and 2012 when they made up a little more than ten percent of the enrollment. This education has made its way back to the mainland as these students take positions as vintners, sommeliers, and other important posts for imparting their knowledge to the benefit of the Chinese wine industry. The proof of their knowledge may be reflected in their sophisticated taste, although it could also mean that Chinese buyers go for top price wines, while knowing little about the wine in the bottle. However, this becomes less likely as larger portions of the population educate themselves about wine. The fact of the matter is that China ranks around twentieth in per capita consumption; it stands at fourth in the value of wine consumed.[181]

This not only means that there will be more knowledge that will inevitably contribute to continued improvement in domestically

---

[181] Wilson T. Vorndick, "China's New Obsession: French Wine," *The New York Times*, December 20, 2017, sec. Opinion, https://www.nytimes.com/2014/01/26/opinion/sunday/chinas-new-obsession-french-wine.html.

produced Chinese wine, but it means that there will be more variation of imports. It is notable to mention that Spain tripled its exports to China between 2011 and 2014.[182] Aside from Old World standbys—France, Spain, and Italy—which remain popular in China, there is an increasing demand for wines from the New World. Although Chile has long been a popular supplier to China and currently ranks third as a supplier to that market, Australia is now the second most popular supplier of wine to China behind France.[183] Why is the relationship between Australia and China so solid? Sommelier Yang Lu offers this insight: "We are still in the young age of our wine market, so the warmness and ripeness of their wines appeals. Out of all of the New World producing countries, Australia is the most interesting."[184]

The Next Half Century of Chinese Wine

Now that we have explored how electronic and mobile commerce may impact Chinese wine consumption habits in the near future, we can turn our attention to the more distant future.

The value of wine consumed in China is growing and is projected to increase to $23 billion in 2021, which will increase by about one-third

---

[182] Jancis Robinson, "Spain Leapfrogs France and Italy," Jancis Robinson, March 29, 2014, https://www.jancisrobinson.com/articles/spain-leapfrogs-france-and-italy.

[183] Sylvia Wu, "Exporting Wine to China: The Top 10 Countries," *Decanter*, February 9, 2018, http://www.decanter.com/wine-news/exporting-wine-to-china-countries-384383/.

[184] Lyons, "The People's Republic of Wine", 2-3.

since 2016 ($15.24 billion). China's consumption volume is projected to reach 192 million 9-liter cases in the same span. Demand will continue to outsize the production, and premium wine will figure heavily into the equation, making China a valuable import market. These numbers are telling, but the growth is not nearly as astonishing as what is projected to happen in the next fifty years.[185]

In 2008, Berry Bros. & Rudd, Britain's oldest wine and spirits merchant which is based in London, released their Future of Wine report which took modern trends and projected what the industry would look like in 2058. Interestingly, they found that climate change will be a major factor in the future of wine production with the biggest loser being Australia. Australians have battled for years with drought and rising temperatures to continue producing world-class wine. The report predicted that China would transform into the world's wine superpower, expecting the number of vineyards in the nation to increase tenfold. About a quarter of these vineyards are predicted to specialize in fine wine that Master of Wine Jasper Morris asserts will "rival the best of Bordeaux." He speculated: "It is entirely conceivable that, in such a vast country, there will be pockets of land with a terroir and micro-climate well suited to the production of good quality wines."[186]

---

[185] Vinexpo Newsroom, "Powerful China Poised to Drive World Wine Growth," *Vinexpo Newsroom - Wine & Spirits News by Vinexpo* (blog), February 8, 2018, https://www.vinexpo-newsroom.com/powerful-china-poised-drive-world-wine-growth/.

[186] Oliver Styles, "China to Become Leading Wine Producer?," *Decanter*, May 9, 2008, http://www.decanter.com/wine-news/china-to-become-leading-wine-producer-82458/.

So what is the final word on the future of China? The director of Berry Bros. & Rudd, Alun Griffiths, believes that "China has the vineyards, but not the technical expertise." He adds, "However, if good people from wine-producing countries think there is an opportunity to make wine in China, they will go there and invest."[187] There is no longer speculation because, as has been well chronicled here and in other volumes, perhaps most significantly in *Thirsty Dragon*, the French (who are considered by many along with the majority of Chinese oenophiles to be the premier winemakers of the world) continue to invest significant resources into the Chinese wine industry. So, when asking the question will China likely be a contender in producing fine wine? The answer: a resounding Yes! And Jasper Morris agrees, stating; "I absolutely think China will be a fine wine player rivaling the best wines from France."[188]

Currently, there is still a significant gap between the quality of wine produced in China and that of Bordeaux or even Napa Valley. However, all indications are that the gap is slowly closing with regards to quality. This begs the question, where would China be if they produced wine on that level? This possibility might not be too far from becoming a reality.

Due to the fact that Chinese wines are now starting to win awards and receive favorable ratings from top wine influencers, Chinese wine will be exported in greater quantities. Sommelier Noel Shu asserts that it

---

[187] James Meikle, "Chateau China, a Taste of Wines to Come with Climate Change," *The Guardian*, May 8, 2008, sec. Environment, http://www.theguardian.com/environment/2008/may/09/food.fooddrinks.

[188] Styles, "China to Become Leading Wine Producer?"

is only a matter of time until "you'll be seeing Chinese wine stocked at restaurants in New York and London which is almost impossible to find today." He reminds us that in the past it was hard to find regions with "up-and-coming wine industries," but now wines from places like South Africa and Chile can be found almost everywhere and whatever stigmas that might have been once attached to wines from these regions have all but melted away over time. China will be no different. He is confident that all it will require is "a few flagship brands with exceptional quality for China to compete with high-end brands in the international arena." Shu reflects what many predict which is that "the Chinese wine industry will continue to evolve and, one day, may show the world incredible wines that even the toughest critics will praise and enjoy."[189]

The Ascent of Sparkling and White Wine

Some Chinese people have prejudices against the color white because it is often associated with death, whereas red is considered the most auspicious color in China, contributing to a bias toward red wine. As a result, red wine is somewhere between 80 and 90 percent of the wine consumed in China. However, a deeper look at the tastes of Chinese consumers might reveal the future of consumption patterns in China. In an article entitled "China loves red wine, but white may become more popular", Chinese wine enthusiast and blogger Jim Boyce states that he has conducted numerous blind taste tests over a

---

[189] Shu, *China Through a Glass of Wine*, 125-126.

five-year period and found that "inexpensive whites receive equal, if not higher, scores than their red counterparts." Moreover, he cites the blind tastings that Professor Ma Huiqin of China Agricultural University had conducted annually with her classes over a twelve-year period and found that they preferred white twice as much as red wines. He concludes that it is unlikely that whites will actually outsell reds, but that the change in the market "could still add up to hundreds of millions of bottles."[190]

Author of *China Through a Glass of Wine*, sommelier Noel Shu, predicts that white wine will be the rage of the future in China because the lighter and sweeter characteristics that generally define white wine are more in tune with the Chinese palate.[191] White wine has been subject to some resistance for several reasons, most notably the infatuation with Bordeaux's reds which helped initiate the wine craze in China, elevating the importance of red wine in the mind of many. Additionally, that red, the color of the PRC, is associated with luck whereas white is considered unlucky because of the association of that color with death. Chris Ruffle believes that white wine will take a greater market share as "restaurants have more capability to chill whites, and consumers get to know how well whites can pair with many Chinese dishes."[192]

---

[190] Jim Boyce, "China Loves Red Wine, but White May Become More Popular," *South China Morning Post*, November 27, 2014, http://www.scmp.com/lifestyle/food-wine/article/1650018/china-loves-red-wine-white-may-become-more-popular.

[191] Shu, *China Through a Glass of Wine*, 22.

[192] Ruffle, *A Decent Bottle of Wine in China*, 152.

So, the ascent of white wine is imminent, especially considering the ballooning popularity of sparkling white wine. As Shu notes, "With the Chinese market maturing and becoming more knowledgeable about wine, white wine is gaining a newfound preference among savvy consumers."[193]

Speaking of newfound preferences, one of the growing trends in the Chinese wine industry is sparkling wine. Sparkling wine in China produced in China is a new phenomenon. Louis Vuitton Moet Hennessy (LVMH) chose to open Chandon China, the nation's first sparkling wine house, in 2013. The winery is a joint venture with a Chinese company which invested a total of $28 million in the project with LVMH. The group has other houses devoted to sparkling wine spread throughout the globe including Brazil, California, and Australia. However, the Chinese project is special because it was the first piece in this rapidly growing industry, and it has helped to give sparkling wine an elevated image and more profound presence in the world's fastest growing wine market.

China was the world's largest consumer of red wine by 2014 and most experts project that trend to continue; it is just a matter of how significant the increase will be. For example, Euromonitor International projects an 82.4% growth between 2015 and 2020.[194] But what will the fate of sparkling wine be?

---

[193] Shu, *China Through a Glass of Wine*, 22.

[194] Thibaud, "Sparkling Wine in China: Will Demand Match Supply?," Daxue Consulting, June 20, 2016, http://daxueconsulting.com/sparkling-wine-in-china-will-demand-match-supply/.

There was a recent boom in sparkling wine consumption in China; the total increase in volume of sparkling wine in China between 2010 and 2015 has been an eye-popping 352.7%. But this might have been due to the fact that sparkling wine was not as much of a target during the 2012 government crackdown as the conspicuous consumption of elite Bordeaux reds. Also, the push by LVMH and other domestic producers of sparkling wine seems to have sparked a fad, which might not be well aligned with the tastes of Chinese wine consumers. As a result, the consumption of sparkling wine has stagnated and is predicted to drop in the near future. Euromonitor International foresees a 6.9% drop in consumption between 2015 and 2020. [195]

The takeaway is that regardless of the fluctuations in the sparkling wine market, the non-sparkling market will continue to grow in consumption. The recent spike in sparkling wine shows that there is a greater openness to trying new wines in China. Many Chinese wine experts like Noel Shu and Jim Boyce see the possibility of white wine gaining popularity. Logically, the more options that consumers have, the more likely individuals are to find something that will fit their palates. This bodes well for the future of the Chinese wine industry, which is projected to become the world's largest market sometime in the next decade.

---

[195] Ibid.

China's Infatuation with Icewine

The 2018 Decanter Awards was the best ever for Chinese wineries. China captured 183 seals of approval and medals, which more than doubled their awards from 2017. Perhaps the most interesting winner was Changyu's "Golden Icewine Valley Blue Label Vidal" from Liaoning. Several other icewines also received silver or bronze medals. This is an indication of the improvements in icewine production in China.[196]

Icewine has become increasingly popular. The process of these wines is unique; grapes that grow in cold climates are allowed to freeze by harvesting them later in the season (or they are purposely frozen to simulate this process). The result is that the grapes produce a wine with a higher sugar content which tends to be more viscous. This process is expensive and the yield is lower than traditionally produced wines, driving the price up.

The quality of icewines produced is partially a reflection of the increasing popularity of icewine in China. Icewines have become so popular that demand is outpacing production. Therefore, China has looked to traditional icewine-producing countries to import more. Canada produces some of the best icewines in the world due to cold temperatures and strict regulations including the requirement that the grapes freeze naturally on the vine and are not harvested early and

---

[196] Sylvia Wu, "China Wins Eight Gold Medals at 2018 Decanter World Wine Awards," *Decanter China,* May 29, 2018, https://www.decanterchina.com/en/news/china-wins-eight-gold-medals-at-2018-decanter-world-wine-awards.

cryogenically frozen. This creates a stable and authentic product, something that Chinese wine consumers crave. Although red wines are still king in China, icewines are challenging that statistic. There are many sweet wines that are pleasing to the Chinese palate, and this makes icewine a natural fit in China. Once icewine was introduced to China in the early 2000s, it was a hit. Between 2004 and 2011, Canadian icewine exports to China increased nearly fifteen-fold. Although the blistering pace of icewine imports has slowed since the boom, icewines continue to be popular in China.[197]

So, demand continues to outstrip the supply, causing Chinese wineries to scramble, producing more icewine to fill the gap. This also has opened the door to counterfeiting, which has flourished in the icewine market. When Randy Dufour, Vice President of Global Travel Retail for Constellation Brands, visited wine stores and stores specializing in high-end Canadian products such as maple syrup and icewine, he stated, "You go to some of these stores and there's fifty or sixty brands of icewine and maybe five or ten of them are legitimate." This not only cuts into the legitimate product margins, but it might turn off a potential customer trying icewine for the first time and getting a poor imitation. From Dufour's perspective, "It's quite frightening."[198]

---

[197] Trevor Cole, "Asia's Favourite Canadian Export," *The Globe and Mail*, March 27, 2013, https://www.theglobeandmail.com/report-on-business/rob-magazine/asias-favourite-canadian-export/article10311708/.

[198] Ibid.

Other Factors Affecting the Future of Chinese Wine Production

In 2018, the projection of wine production globally is estimated to be decreased by 20%. There are many factors to the new wine shortage that we are currently in the grips of. There are political factors beyond the unpredictability of President Trump's direction with tariffs and economic policies and the threat of the new trade war with China which will have global wine implications. There is the looming uncertainty of Brexit (the British exit vote from the European Union) and other movements within the EU that can impact the industry. But the greatest issue is climate change. This has caused low yields in locations across the globe with wildfires deeply damaging areas of California as well as locations in the Iberian Peninsula, with producers in the Southern Hemisphere being hit the hardest. For many locations in the Southern Hemisphere, 2017 will be the worst yield in a generation, and in other areas the worst since 1945. As Mike Veseth, professor emeritus of International Political Economy at the University of Puget Sound and editor of *The Wine Economist*, points out, "The impact on the global market will be significant...it could be game-changing." He refers to this situation as the "Big Squeeze."[199]

---

[199] Mike Veseth, "Mother Nature Strikes Back: The Big Wine Market Squeeze of 2018," *The Wine Economist* (blog), January 9, 2018, https://wineeconomist.com/2018/01/09/big-squeeze/.

He asserts that the Big Three producers (Italy, France, and Spain) stand to lose the most in the Big Squeeze. Additionally, other major production areas such as California and Australia also had sub-par harvests, mostly due to climate-related issues. Not only will they have a dip in production but some of the producers will also have a worse margin, which might cause bulk wine to migrate up the supply chain and into bottles at a higher price point. This could present opportunities for mass producers of wine as well as producers of mid-level wines that are overlooked in years with higher yields.[200]

This could present opportunities for Chinese winemakers who will be more competitive in their domestic market against countries like Australia and Spain from which they have traditionally purchased large quantities of bulk wine. Moreover, it could make the few mid-level wines that China exports more competitive, leading to increased sales and possibly better margins for Chinese producers. One man's disaster is another's opportunity.

The other interesting aspect for China is that the country is so vast that it is comprised of many starkly different climates. Therefore, as the weather patterns continue to shift due to global warming, there will inevitably be parts of China where the wine industry is unaffected, allowing China to continue to grow its production while small countries with less diversity will suffer, causing countries like Australia to lose ground.

---

[200] Mike Veseth, "Trickle Up Wine Economics and the Big Wine Market Squeeze of 2018," *The Wine Economist* (blog), January 16, 2018, https://wineeconomist.com/2018/01/16/trickle-up/.

The Future of the United States and Chinese Wines

Donald Trump is rapidly changing the world order and how people do business throughout the world amazingly. His changes have impacted many industries, including the Chinese wine industry.

In early 2018, Trump started a trade war with China. In the midst of this salvo, China slapped a tariff on wines coming from the United States. In 2017, the United States ranked sixth in terms of volume of wine imported by China.[201] This volume translated to $82 million of wine sent to China (not including duty-free wine entering Hong Kong). It is important to note that this represents a 700% increase over the past ten years.[202]

This disarray has opened new opportunities for countries like Australia who are competing with the US to export their wine to China. China has now become Australia's largest trading partner. Wine continues to be a large part of the equation. 2017 was a record year for Australia as they saw a 15% increase in the value of wine exported to $2.56 billion. China's share increased 63% over the previous year to the tune of $848 million. Contrast that figure with about $80 million of wine flowing from the US to China.[203]

---

[201] Wu, "Exporting Wine to China."

[202] Natalie Kitroeff, "China Finds California Wine Pairs Well With a Trade War," *The New York Times*, April 3, 2018, sec. Business Day, https://www.nytimes.com/2018/04/03/business/economy/china-wine-trade.html.

[203] Scott Neuman, "Who Wins A U.S.-China Trade War? Maybe Australia," NPR.org, April 3, 2018, https://www.npr.org/sections/thetwo-way/2018/04/03/599081151/who-wins-a-u-s-china-trade-war-maybe-australia.

Robert P. Koch, president and CEO of the Wine Institute, asserts that the tariff imposed by China "will have a chilling effect on U.S. wine exports to one of the world's most important markets," and he concludes that "U.S. producers were already at a disadvantage to many foreign competitors, and this will only exacerbate that problem. We urge a swift resolution to this crisis before long-term damage is done to the U.S. wine industry."[204]

Conversely, China imports so little U.S. wine to begin with that it will have a minute impact on their wine economy. So the tariffs not only pose a problem for U.S. winemakers who have spent years and in some cases more than a decade trying to make inroads for their products in China, but they will also represent an opportunity for other countries that will increase their market share as consumption continues to increase, where they are projected to eclipse all other nations besides the U.S. by 2020.

---

[204] Jeff Daniels, "China Tariff Hit for US Agriculture Could Be Big Gain for Australia," CNBC.com, April 2, 2018, https://www.cnbc.com/2018/04/02/china-tariff-hit-for-us-agriculture-could-be-big-gain-for-australia.html..

CHAPTER X

Conclusion

China is a country with an ancient history and long-established traditions. China has a rich history of wine production that dates back millenia. These cultural heritages from tea ceremonies to the appreciation of alcohol primed China for the rapid expansion of wine appreciation and the wine industry at the end of the twentieth century.

Although China has significant traditions with regards to rice wine, spirits, and beer, the modern wine industry was slow to develop. The arrival of *Vitis Vinifera* in 138 BCE was one of the quiet moments in history that had a major unforeseen impact far later. Softly, the noble grape seeped into Chinese society evidenced by poetry and oral tradition.

Not until the dream of tycoon Chang Bishi was realized at the close of the nineteenth century did modern winemaking techniques take hold in China, laying the groundwork for a fledgling industry to grow. When Chairman Mao established the People's Republic of China in 1949, a marked shift in the Chinese socioeconomic system ushered in profound changes to many facets of life in China. The transition from Mao's philosophies to the market economy of Deng Xioping set the table for the economic growth that would foster the development of the wine industry.

The love for wine grew slowly in China with the early mavens enjoying bottles of Bordeaux, shaping China's Francophile wine culture. Importantly, Li Peng's proclamation in 1996 added significant momentum to China's growing wine industry and encouraged Chinese people to seek wine as the preferred alcoholic beverage for gifting and social lubrication for the first time. The result, as we have seen, was staggering growth of wine imports and the domestic wine industry that continues today in the face of climate change and other market forces that have slowed the global wine industry.

Counterfeiting and other trappings of the industry's success would follow. But nothing would be able to mute China's rise in prominence as a major player in the global wine scene. Today, China is ripe for adventure and increasingly, oenophiles are visiting China to experience the growth of this powerful industry and to discover a new twist on an old celebrated indulgence.

As the Romans lighted on this important truth which can be traced back to the poetry of Alcaeus, "*In Vino Veritas*" (In Wine Truth), there is a great deal of truth that can be found in China while gazing at the country through a bottle of wine. The future is a mystery, but by drinking deeply from China's rich past, one can be sated with rich rewards.

China still faces rampant poverty in the countryside, which is one reason that President Xi has promised to move 100 million rural Chinese to cities by 2020. This is part of his broader initiative to combat poverty in China. Wine in China offers many opportunities for various sectors of society. Aside from the wealthy, Chinese entrepreneurs who are making money importing and exporting wine, opening vineyards, and designing apps, the noble grape offers something for the impoverished workers in the countryside. With crippling poverty in many rural areas where the wine industry is growing, the noble grape is a symbol of hope. This is a unifying theme in China, that wine is the way to a better life whether profiting from some part of the industry or as a symbol of status, or experiencing pleasure, prosperity, and friendship.

It is an important reminder that the globe is more connected than ever, and nothing as significant as the development of wine in China happens in a vacuum. We live in a global society, and wine is a shared drink that has meaning throughout—what one culture does affects the others—wine should be a binding experience because the true oenophiles appreciate the effort and sophistication in creating a fine wine that is meant ultimately to be enjoyed. This new chapter of wine in China will continue to reshape the global wine industry and Chinese society. For those who follow the story, China will continue to astound.

APPENDIX

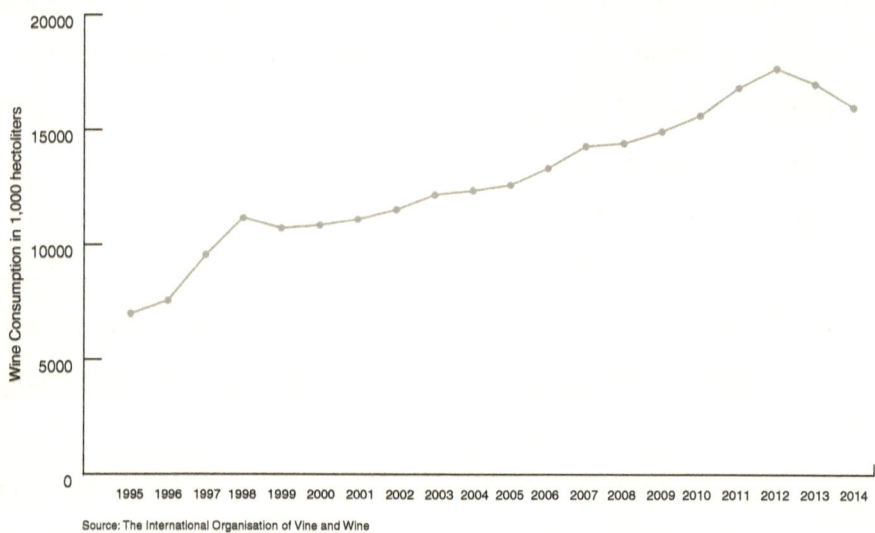

Figure 1. Wine Consumption Volume in China from 1995 to 2014 (in 1,000 hectoliters)

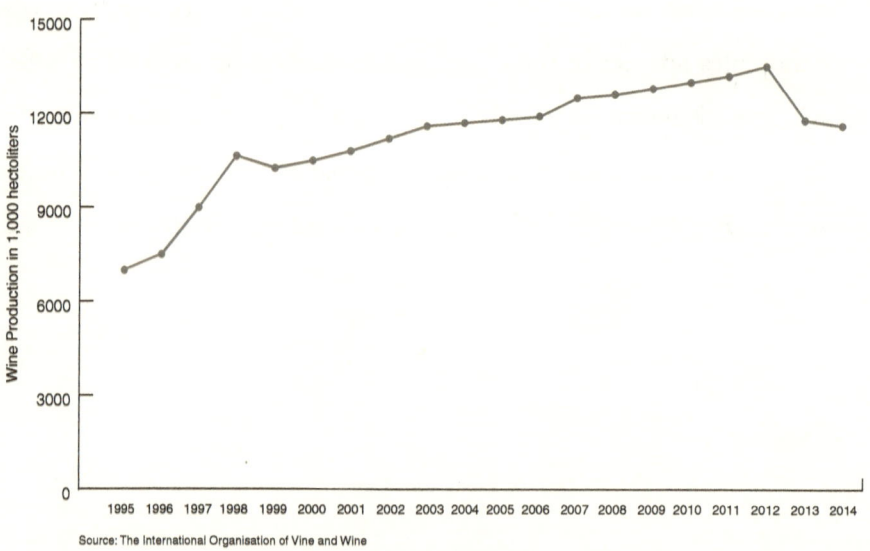

Figure 2. Wine Production Volume in China from 1995 to 2014 (in 1,000 hectoliters)

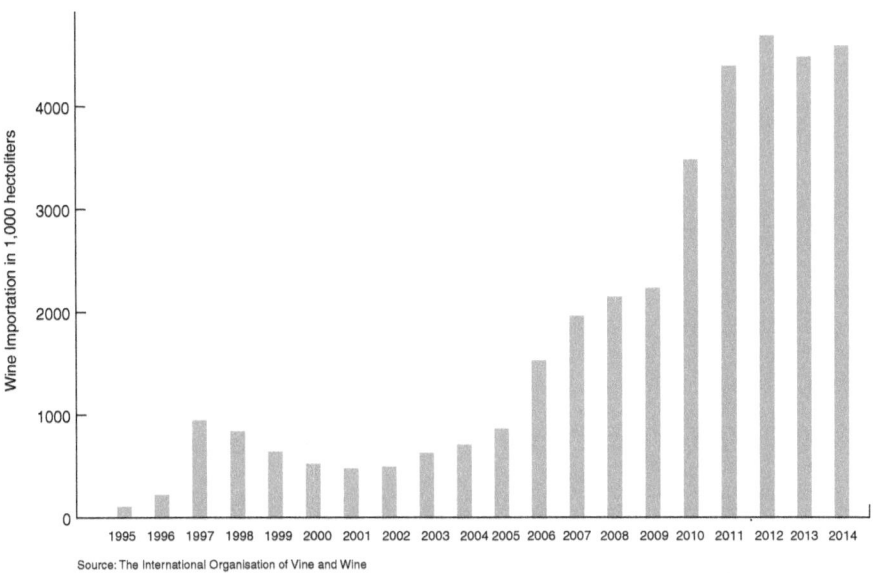

Figure 3. Wine Importation Volume in China from 1995 to 2014 (in 1,000 hectoliters)

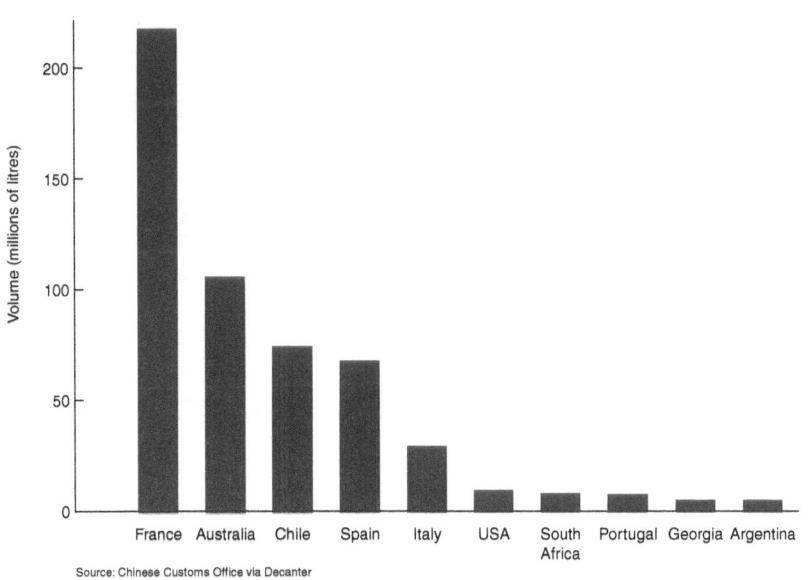

Figure 4. The Source of China's Wine Imports in 2017

Bibliography

Agence France-Presse. "'China Will Rock Our Wine World' But Needs Time." *Wine-Searcher*, June 2, 2014. https://www.wine-searcher.com/m/2014/06/china-will-rock-our-wine-world.

———. "China's Anti-Bling Push Hits French Wine Exports." *Wine-Searcher*, September 10, 2014. https://www.wine-searcher.com/m/2014/09/china-s-anti-bling-push-hits-french-wine-exports.

———. "Chinese Corruption Crackdown, Bad Harvest Leads to Bordeaux Wine Sales Fall." *The Guardian*, March 20, 2015, sec. World news. http://www.theguardian.com/world/2015/mar/20/chinese-corruption-crackdown-bad-harvest-leads-to-bordeaux-wine-sales-fall.

Akalin, Can, and Lawrence Lazar. *Wine in China: Insights on a Burgeoning Industry in an e/m Commerce Context*. 2nd edition. CreateSpace Independent Publishing Platform, 2015.

Bibliography

Alfonsi, Sharyn. "Billionaire Koch Brother's Crusade against Counterfeit Wine." CBS News, October 22, 2017. https://www.cbsnews.com/news/billionaire-koch-brothers-crusade-against-counterfeit-wine/.

Baker, Aryn. "The Sweet Taste of Success." *Time*, May 16, 2005. http://content.time.com/time/subscriber/article/0,33009,1059080,00.html.

Balazovic, Todd. "Wine Growers Go Online to Boost Sales." *China Daily Europe*, March 7, 2014. http://europe.chinadaily.com.cn/epaper/2014-03/07/content_17329583.htm.

Boyce, Jim. "Beijing Bob: Dinner with Robert Parker on the Great Wall of China." *Grape Wall of China*, June 6, 2008. http://www.grapewallofchina.com/2008/06/06/robert-parker-wine-dinner-china/.

———. "China Loves Red Wine, but White May Become More Popular." *South China Morning Post*, November 27, 2014. http://www.scmp.com/lifestyle/food-wine/article/1650018/china-loves-red-wine-white-may-become-more-popular.

———. "Wine Word - Robert Parker in Beijing." *Grape Wall of China*, May 27, 2008. http://www.grapewallofchina.com/2008/05/27/robert-parker-beijing-china-wine-tasting/.

"China Makes Big Bet on Turning Desert into Wine Region." CBS News, January 1, 2016. https://www.cbsnews.com/news/china-aims-become-top-wine-producer-ningxia-region-vineyards/.

Chow, Jason. "China Is Now World's Biggest Consumer of Red Wine." *WSJ* (blog), January 29, 2014. https://blogs.wsj.com/scene/2014/01/29/china-is-now-worlds-biggest-consumer-of-red-wine/.

Cole, Trevor. "Asia's Favourite Canadian Export." *The Globe and Mail*, March 27, 2013. https://www.theglobeandmail.com/report-on-business/rob-magazine/asias-favourite-canadian-export/article10311708/.

Daniels, Jeff. "China Tariff Hit for US Agriculture Could Be Big Gain for Australia." CNBC.com, April 2, 2018. https://www.cnbc.com/2018/04/02/china-tariff-hit-for-us-agriculture-could-be-big-gain-for-australia.html.

Dhiraj, Amarendra Bhushan. "World's 15 Richest Cities In 2017: New York, London, And Tokyo, Tops List." *CEOWORLD Magazine* (blog), February 12, 2018. http://ceoworld.biz/2018/02/12/worlds-15-richest-cities-in-2017-new-york-london-and-tokyo-tops-list/.

Eads, Lauren. "China's Taste for Imported Wines Doubles." *The Drinks Business* (blog), June 30, 2014. https://www.thedrinksbusiness.com/2014/06/chinas-taste-for-imported-wines-doubles/.

Eijkhoff, Pieter. *Wine in China: Its History and Contemporary Developments*. Utrecht: P. Eijkhoff : Nederlands Wijngilde, 2000. http://www.eykhoff.nl/Wine%20in%20China.pdf.

Elkins, Kathleen. "There Are More Billionaires in the US than in China, Germany and India Combined." CNBC.com, May 15, 2018. https://uk.finance.yahoo.com/news/more-billionaires-us-china-germany-165900809.html.

Ferdman, Roberto A. "China Now Guzzles More Red Wine than Any Other Country in the World." *Quartz* (blog), February 1, 2014. https://qz.com/172874/china-now-guzzles-more-red-wine-than-any-other-country-in-the-world/.

Fisher, Daniel. "Inside The Koch Empire: How The Brothers Plan To Reshape America." *Forbes*, December 5, 2012. https://www.forbes.com/sites/danielfisher/2012/12/05/inside-the-koch-empire-how-the-brothers-plan-to-reshape-america/.

FlorCruz, Michelle. "China's Wine Industry Explodes, But Not Yet On The World Stage." *International Business Times*, May 3, 2015. http://www.ibtimes.com/chinas-wine-industry-explodes-not-yet-world-stage-1902284.

Francis, Diane. "China's Anti-Corruption Crackdown Threatens to Spill over into Canada." *Financial Post*, August 8, 2014. https://business.financialpost.com/opinion/chinas-anti-corruption-crackdown-threatens-to-spill-over-into-canada.

Friefelder, Jack. "China's Wine Consumption Is Growing." *China Daily USA*, April 4, 2014. http://usa.chinadaily.com.cn/epaper/2014-04/25/content_17465188.htm.

Friefelder, Jack, and Bian Jibu. "Wine in the US: 'Made in China' Is Rare." China Daily USA, October 30, 2015. http://usa.chinadaily.com.cn/epaper/2015-10/30/content_22325719.htm.

Glass of Bubbly. "Angelina, New Sparkling Wine from Grace Vineyard in China." *Glass Of Bubbly* (blog), August 28, 2015. https://www.glassofbubbly.com/angelina-new-sparkling-wine-from-grace-vineyard-in-china/.

"GraceVineyard." Accessed June 27, 2018. http://en.grace-vineyard.com/.

"Hong Kong`s Wine Market with Prospects Until 2017." *Vinexpo Asia-Pacific*, May 2014. http://studylib.net/doc/7694851/hong-kong-s-wine-market-with-prospects-until-2017--source.

Jenner, W. J. F. *The Tyranny of History: The Roots of China's Crisis*. Penguin History. London ; New York: Penguin Books, 1992.

Johnson, Hugh. *Vintage: The Story of Wine*. New York: Simon and Schuster, 1989.

Kitroeff, Natalie. "China Finds California Wine Pairs Well With a Trade War." *The New York Times*, April 3, 2018, sec. Business Day.

https://www.nytimes.com/2018/04/03/business/economy/china-wine-trade.html.

Kwok, Man-Ho, and Joanne O'Brien, eds. *The Eight Immortals of Taoism: Legends and Fables of Popular Taoism*. New York, N.Y., U.S.A: Meridian, 1991.

Lavin, Kate. "The Slow Boat to China." *Wines & Vines*, January 2012. http://www.winesandvines.com/features/95708.

Li, Zhengping. *Chinese Wine: Universe in a Bottle*. Cultural China Series. New York: Cambridge University Press, 2011.

Lichine, Alexis, and William Fifield. *Alexis Lichine's New Encyclopedia of Wines & Spirits*. 5th ed., rev. New York: Knopf, 1987.

Lovemoney Staff. "The Countries with the Most Millionaires Revealed." MSN, June 20, 2017. https://www.msn.com/en-in/news/other/the-countries-with-the-most-millionaires-revealed/ss-BBzsCIg.

Lyons, Will. "The People's Republic of Wine." *Wall Street Journal*, February 7, 2014, sec. Europe. https://www.wsj.com/articles/the-people8217s-republic-of-wine-1391736358.

MacNeil, Karen. *The Wine Bible*. Revised Second Edition. New York: Workman Publishing Co, 2015.

McCoy, Elin. "Top Chinese Wines Have Gone From Bad to Good. Will They Become Great?" *Bloomberg.Com*, June 26, 2015.

https://www.bloomberg.com/news/articles/2015-06-26/top-chinese-wines-have-gone-from-bad-to-good-will-they-become-great-.

Meikle, James. "Chateau China, a Taste of Wines to Come with Climate Change." *The Guardian*, May 8, 2008, sec. Environment. http://www.theguardian.com/environment/2008/may/09/food.fooddrinks.

Moore, Malcolm. "Hong Kong Becomes World's Largest Wine Market." *The Daily Telegraph*, October 6, 2009, sec. Food and Drink. https://www.telegraph.co.uk/foodanddrink/wine/6264679/Hong-Kong-becomes-worlds-largest-wine-market.html.

Moore, Victoria. "A Bottle of Beijing, Please: Is Chinese Wine Any Good?" *The Daily Telegraph*, April 28, 2015, sec. Food and Drink. https://www.telegraph.co.uk/foodanddrink/wine/11568849/A-bottle-of-Beijing-please-is-Chinese-wine-any-good.html.

Mustacich, Suzanne. *Thirsty Dragon: China's Lust for Bordeaux and the Threat to the World's Best Wines*. First edition. New York: Henry Holt and Company, 2015.

Neuman, Scott. "Who Wins A U.S.-China Trade War? Maybe Australia." NPR.org, April 3, 2018. https://www.npr.org/sections/thetwo-way/2018/04/03/599081151/who-wins-a-u-s-china-trade-war-maybe-australia.

Paramaguru, Kharunya. "How China Became the Wine World's Most Unlikely Superpower." *Time*, October 31, 2013. http://business.time.com/2013/10/31/how-china-became-the-wine-worlds-most-unlikely-superpower/.

Puckette, Madeline. "Updated: Top Wine Producing Countries." *Wine Folly*, March 25, 2015. https://winefolly.com/update/top-wine-producing-countries/.

"Rare Wine Dealer Sentenced in Counterfeiting Scheme." Story. Federal Bureau of Investigation, September 5, 2014. https://www.fbi.gov/news/stories/rare-wine-dealer-sentenced-in-counterfeiting-scheme.

"Robert Parker Wine Advocate Announces: New Reviewer In China And New Office In Napa." Charles Communications Associates, December 17, 2015. http://www.charlescomm.com/Big-News/robert-parker-wine-advocate-announces--new-reviewer-in-china-and-new-office-in-napa.html.

Robinson, Jancis. "Big Award for WSET." Jancis Robinson, April 21, 2015. https://www.jancisrobinson.com/articles/big-award-for-wset.

———. "Chinese Wine - Catching up Fast." Jancis Robinson, April 5, 2014. https://www.jancisrobinson.com/articles/chinese-wine-catching-up-fast.

———. "Emma Gao - a Story of Wine Today." Jancis Robinson, November 29, 2012. https://www.jancisrobinson.com/articles/emma-gao-a-story-of-wine-today.

———. "Kiwi Wines Please Chinese Palates." Jancis Robinson, March 7, 2016. https://www.jancisrobinson.com/articles/kiwi-wines-please-chinese-palates.

———. "My Chinese Adventures - Part II." Jancis Robinson, February 1, 2004. https://www.jancisrobinson.com/articles/my-chinese-adventures-part-ii.

———. "Spain Leapfrogs France and Italy." Jancis Robinson, March 29, 2014. https://www.jancisrobinson.com/articles/spain-leapfrogs-france-and-italy.

Ruffle, Chris. *A Decent Bottle of Wine in China*. Hong Kong: Earnshaw Books Limited, 2015.

Schafer, Edward H. *The Golden Peaches of Samarkand: A Study of T'ang Exotics*. Berkeley, Calif.: Univ. of California Press, 1963.

Shen, Anqi. "Fake Wine in China." *Asia Dialogue* (blog), January 16, 2017. http://theasiadialogue.com/2017/01/16/fake-wine-in-china/.

Shepard, Wade. "How European Wine Is Now Going To China Aboard Silk Road Trains." *Forbes*, July 23, 2017. https://www.forbes.com/sites/wadeshepard/2017/07/23/europe-on-the-new-silk-road-european-wine-can-now-be-shipped-to-china-by-rail/.

Shu, Noel. *China Through a Glass of Wine*. Cafe con Leche Books, 2016.

Sima, Qian. *Records of the Grand Historian: Han Dynasty I*. Translated by Burton Watson. Rev. ed. Records of Civilization 65. Hong Kong: Columbia Univ. Press Book, 1993.

"State of the Vitiviniculture World Market." International Organisation of Wine and Vine (OIV), April 2018. http://www.oiv.int/public/medias/5958/oiv-state-of-the-vitiviniculture-world-market-april-2018.pdf.

Styles, Oliver. "China to Become Leading Wine Producer?" *Decanter*, May 9, 2008. http://www.decanter.com/wine-news/china-to-become-leading-wine-producer-82458/.

Taber, George M. *A Toast to Bargain Wines: How Innovators, Iconoclasts, and Winemaking Revolutionaries Are Changing the Way the World Drinks*. 1st Scribner ed. New York: Scribner, 2011.

"The Global Wine Industry." New York NY.: Morgan Stanley Research, October 22, 2013. http://gavinquinney.com/wp-content/uploads/2013/11/MS_wine.pdf.

Thibaud. "Sparkling Wine in China: Will Demand Match Supply?" Daxue Consulting, June 20, 2016. http://daxueconsulting.com/sparkling-wine-in-china-will-demand-match-supply/.

US Census Bureau Foreign Trade Division. "Foreign Trade: Data." United States Census Bureau, May 21, 2018. https://www.census.gov/foreign-trade/balance/c5700.html#2001.

Veseth, Mike. "Mother Nature Strikes Back: The Big Wine Market Squeeze of 2018." *The Wine Economist* (blog), January 9, 2018. https://wineeconomist.com/2018/01/09/big-squeeze/.

———. "Trickle Up Wine Economics and the Big Wine Market Squeeze of 2018." *The Wine Economist* (blog), January 16, 2018. https://wineeconomist.com/2018/01/16/trickle-up/.

Vinexpo Newsroom. "China Is a Leading Wine Market of the Future." *Vinexpo Newsroom - Wine & Spirits News by Vinexpo* (blog), April 4, 2017. https://www.vinexpo-newsroom.com/china-is-a-leading-wine-market-of-the-future/.

———. "E-Commerce to Drive Triple Growth for Wine in China." *Vinexpo Newsroom - Wine & Spirits News by Vinexpo* (blog), June 3, 2016. https://www.vinexpo-newsroom.com/e-commerce-to-drive-triple-growth-for-wine-in-china/.

———. "Powerful China Poised to Drive World Wine Growth." *Vinexpo Newsroom - Wine & Spirits News by Vinexpo* (blog), February 8, 2018. https://www.vinexpo-newsroom.com/powerful-china-poised-drive-world-wine-growth/.

Vorndick, Wilson T. "China's New Obsession: French Wine." *The New York Times*, December 20, 2017, sec. Opinion.

https://www.nytimes.com/2014/01/26/opinion/sunday/chinas-new-obsession-french-wine.html.

Wang, Helen H. "The Biggest Story of Our Time: The Rise of China's Middle Class." *Forbes*, December 21, 2011. https://www.forbes.com/sites/helenwang/2011/12/21/the-biggest-story-of-our-time-the-rise-of-chinas-middle-class/.

———. "Two Reasons Chinese Millennials Have More Cash To Burn." Forbes, October 9, 2016. https://www.forbes.com/sites/helenwang/2016/10/09/two-reasons-why-chinese-millennials-have-more-cash-to-burn/.

Wu, Kuo-Cheng. *The Chinese Heritage: A New and Provocative View of the Origins of Chinese Society*. 1st ed. New York: Crown, 1982.

Wu, Sylvia. "China Wins Eight Gold Medals at 2018 Decanter World Wine Awards." *Decanter China*, May 29, 2018. https://www.decanterchina.com/en/news/china-wins-eight-gold-medals-at-2018-decanter-world-wine-awards.

———. "Exporting Wine to China: The Top 10 Countries." *Decanter*, February 9, 2018. http://www.decanter.com/wine-news/exporting-wine-to-china-countries-384383/.

Acknowledgements

A special thank you to my Aunt Vivian Lipari who doggedly helped me to finish the book; she was pivotal in helping me see this project through.

Many thanks to my Uncle Tony Stavely, who was extremely generous in sharing his vast knowledge of wine and bolstering the manuscript with informed suggestions gleaned from his time in China. He has been a tremendous help and continued to send me research throughout the project. I feel so lucky to have him as a friend, mentor, teacher, and as an uncle.

Thank you to Stan Skrabut for helping me get a hold of the footnotes and for continuing to expand my mind with regards to the possibilities of utilizing technology.

Thank you to my mother, who has been a driving force in this project and continues to be a shining light in my life and the ultimate champion of my work.

To my father for his unwavering support no matter what path I choose, even something as unconventional as Chinese wine.

Thank you to my Aunt Mary Mayshark-Stavely for her willingness to help with my work and sharing knowledge that continues to enrich my life.

Deep gratitude to my Aunt Virginia and Grandma Laura who gave me tremendous support as I worked through the book. I know that you will see this come to fruition no matter where you are.

Thank you to the wonderful librarians at the Mayville library, specifically Melissa Bartok and Elizabeth Schmitz, who helped me find valuable resources for the book.

Also, a big thanks to Reta Carden, owner of East Branch Books in Sherman, NY, because she has always been kind and generous especially in meticulously helping me find rare books for this project. Her beautiful bookstore is an amazing place to get lost and a jewel in the community.

I would also like to thank the many educators who helped me acquire the skills necessary to complete a book on such a challenging subject. There are too many to name here but I would like especially to thank Professor Theresa Kelleher for instilling a passion for Chinese history and Asian philosophies in me.

I would also like to thank the Massoud family for giving me an opportunity to work at Paumanok Vineyards.

Thank you to the Mack family, the Salvatore family, Evan and Kyla Bucholz, chefs Michael Ross and Tom Schaudel, Adam Lovett, Eileen Renshaw, and everyone else who aided my journey at the Jedediah Hawkins house and on Long Island in general.

Thank you to the Sandstrom family and all my friends in Sweden for their kindness and support.

Finally, I would like to express my gratitude to the many other friends and family members, too numerous to name here.

About the Author

Loren Mayshark was fortunate to have parents who offered him opportunities to see the world and instilled in him a passion for travel. As his wanderlust grew, he journeyed to more than thirty US states and at least as many foreign countries while visiting four continents.

After college, he supported his itinerant lifestyle by working dozens of jobs, including golf caddy, travel writer, construction worker, fireworks salesman, substitute teacher, and vineyard laborer. Predominantly his jobs have been in the restaurant industry. He cut his teeth as a server, maître d', and bartender at San Francisco's historic Fisherman's Grotto #9, the original restaurant on the Fisherman's Wharf. While working with a colorful crew of primarily Mexican and Chinese co-workers, he gained a passion for Spanish and spent several months wandering through South America, learning the language and immersing himself in the varied landscapes and cultures.

While living in New York City, he attended both the Gotham Writers Workshop and the New York Writers Workshop. He is a regular contributor to Can the Man, an alternative media resource focused on social justice, and The Jovial Journey, a website dedicated to food, drink, and travel. He has written for *The Permaculture Research Institute* and *Uisio* among other prominent outlets.

Loren Mayshark's first book, *Death: An Exploration*, won the 2016 Beverly Hills Book Award in the category of Death and Dying and was a finalist for book of the year in the 2016 Foreword INDIES Awards in the category of Grief/Grieving (Adult Nonfiction).

He received a BA in World History from Manhattanville College in 2004 while minoring in World Religions. He attended the MA History program at Hunter College in Manhattan.

For more information visit his website: lorenmayshark.com.

About The Publisher

Red Scorpion Press was formed in January 2016 with the hope of bettering the world in a small way through publishing. Our aim is to push boundaries and be an outlet for fresh voices and unique perspectives that entertain and inform.

Please visit us at www.redscorpionpress.com for our latest selection of books.

www.ingramcontent.com/pod-product-compliance
Lightning Source LLC
Chambersburg PA
CBHW020423010526
44118CB00010B/397